RITES FOR LIFE
REGENERATE | MASTER ENERGY | TRANSFORM

WITH ANNE LEWIS

ACKNOWLEDGEMENT rites for life

beyond gratitude

It is with all my heart that I wish to thank those who have helped selflessly with the creation of this book.

Thank you John, a dear friend, father of our two extraordinary sons and teacher. Without your wisdom and insight, I would not have had the courage to reveal these additional three Rites. Your ability to see truth and your guidance is beyond words. You have been a pivotal part in bringing this knowledge through me to pass onto humanity.

Thank you Andy, you are a gift to us all for your belief in this work and your genius in creating the stunning design of this book. You have had infinite patience, igniting the fire of action which enabled this book to be. Your endless time and business prowess without any notion of reward has been one of true selfless service. It is an honour to have you by my side.

Thank you Magda, for your dedication and enthusiastic support. Your unconditional friendship, expertise and ethic is truly an example of how a divine being walks on this earth. You have been a godsend of encouragement and without your invaluable help this book would not have been.

Thank you to all those that connected with the energy of our classes and courses over the many years, that have allowed me the growth and experience to present a tool that does and will assist with the evolvement of our spirituality.

Words fall short of the love and appreciation felt to all of you who played a part in this wondrous journey called Rites for Life.

the divine within me honours the divine within you!

RITES FOR LIFE
REGENERATE | MASTER ENERGY | TRANSFORM

Copyright © 2015 Anne Lewis

All rights reserved.

No part of this publication may be reproduced, stored in a retrieval system, or transmitted, in any form or by any means, electronic, mechanical, photocopying, recording or otherwise, without the prior written permission of the author.

The author can be reached at **www.ritesforlife.com**

contents

INTRODUCTION | *Rites for Life*	7
MY JOURNEY | with the *Rites for Life*	11

regenerate   14

CHAPTER 1 \|
Regenerate with energy   16

1. The Physical body — 17
2. The Emotional body — 20
3. The Mental body — 23
4. The Energy body — 25
5. The Spiritual body — 26
6. Clearing the Physical, Emotional and Mental bodies — 27

CHAPTER 2 \|
Healing your chakras   32

Chakra visualisation — 44

master energy   48

CHAPTER 3 \|
The power of I am   51

Wanting and having — 51
Rites for Life - 'I am' Affirming statements — 52

CHAPTER 4 \|
Learning the Rites   60

RITES 1-5   56

Open your heart — 60
RITE 1 Rite for Light - Spinning — 64
RITE 2 Rite for Here - Leg raises — 70
RITE 3 Rite for Love - Back arch — 78
RITE 4 Rite for Strength - Table top — 84
RITE 5 Rite for Flow - Downward/upward facing dog — 90

RITES 6-8   98

RITE 6 Rite for Creation - Standing twist — 100
RITE 7 Rite for Divinity - Headstand — 106
RITE 8 Rite for Joy - Smiling meditation — 112

transform   120

CHAPTER 5 |	Releasing & clearing	122
CHAPTER 6 |	Abundant health	129
CHAPTER 7 |	Tips & considerations	134
CHAPTER 8 |	Embracing your ego	140
CHAPTER 9 |	Your heart's purpose	146
CHAPTER 10 |	Rites for Life program	151
CHAPTER 11 |	Case studies	154

introducing rites for life

Many spiritual teachers speak about the importance of being guided by your heart, living in the moment and meditating, yet how do you do this? For the past three decades I have been teaching the Rites for Life around the world to thousands of people. I have found the Rites to be the most profoundly healing tool that opens your heart, stills the mind, creates greater awareness and heals the body.

The *Rites for Life* consists of eight simple yogic exercises that you practise daily. Many of you may know of the five Tibetan Rites. The *Rites for Life* include these five exercises with an additional three Rites to complete the practice. The Rites were developed many thousands of years ago as a healing and cleansing tool and were passed down through the generations. The ancients were aware that the mind and body needed to be cleansed so that they could work to raise spiritual consciousness. The purpose of their life was to gain and maintain a higher level of consciousness not only for their own development but also for the development of humanity.

Today the *Rites for Life* are tools that are available for our use and benefit. The *Rites for Life* strengthen and tone the body very quickly. They also create greater flexibility and work to heal disease and discomfort. In yoga philosophy it is recognised that the mind, body and emotions are connected, so the exercises not only improve the health of the body, they also allow the emotions to be more stable and the mind to be clearer and more focused.

When the body, emotions and mind are in balance, then we can have a greater understanding and awareness of our own spiritual nature. It is like peeling away the layers of stress and tension on all levels in order to be in touch with the heart. In yoga we consider the heart centre to be the seat of the higher self.

In essence the *Rites for Life* are tools that help us surrender all that stands in the way of our true purpose in life. No matter what you do, who you are or where you live, your purpose in life is to grow spiritually and to be the best that you can. The *Rites for Life* will enable you to do exactly that. This ancient energetic ritual allows us to connect to the inner wisdom of the heart. As a spiritual teacher I am aware of the importance of being guided by the heart, living in the moment and having a purposeful life.

Yet how do you do this? By practising the *Rites for Life*.

The subtleties, modifications and precautions that are necessary for a safe and successful practice are included in this book. Regardless of age, fitness levels or your circumstances in life these transformational tools are here now.

The Rites for Life keep the body healthy, strong, flexible and balanced. We are able to transform physical, emotional and mental imbalances, allowing for an unobstructed path to our divine purpose. My purpose was discovered through adversity and this led me to search for ways of greater awareness and health. The Rites were revealed to me in a vision and further instruction was provided many years later that there were another three.

Immediately, I started to practise them with a healthy skepticism and excitement. I tested them and tested them some more and found that my energies on all levels were greatly heightened. My life shifted dramatically and since then I have had the privilege of introducing the ritual to many other people. Observing the growth in people doing the additional three proved to me that they were powerful and were here to help us in this day and age. I witnessed profound energy shifts and cellular regeneration. People expressed a magical transformation of their minds and emotions, as well as enhanced flexibility, a stronger body, and a feeling of being healthier and looking younger.

Intuitively, I still felt that there was something more. In contemplative meditation I developed a significant complement to the practice. The 'I am' consciousness has been introduced in later chapters to help with the focus and ease of the practice. This tool is profound and uses the power of the 'I am' to remind us of universal truth which leads us to higher consciousness.

The key to success with the *Rites for Life* is to do the practice daily and slowly working up to the complete practice over 30 weeks. By week 30 you are practising about 40-60 minutes a day, which includes yoga, relaxation and meditation.

The Rites for Life are an evolution. Now, the ritual is complete. An advanced and evolved practice has come to be! As human beings we have progressed and it is only natural to take this next step.

It is extremely exciting when we start to feel more energy, which the Rites promote. This added energy in yogic terms is called prana. Prana is a sanskrit word for "life force". This life force is healing on all levels and it is this life force that is largely responsible for the healing and transformative process.

Welcome to the beginning of a life full of joy, purpose, greater health and awareness. Remember that as you work on yourself you will be contributing to the planet and all of her inhabitants. So let's get started with a great sense of joy and a deep gratitude to the ancients for their wisdom and the tools that have been passed down to us.

my journey with the rites for life

This book was inspired by the most powerful transformational ritual that was born out of a soul's search and destiny to regenerate, master energy and transform. I have always had a deep longing and inner knowing that there had to be ways to live life without suffering. That it is possible to live a life with an abundance of health, a greater connection to universal wisdom and to master healing energy. Essentially, we can transform from a state of deep sadness to one of joy and love.

As with most of us, transformations and awakenings occur when life presents us with devastating challenges that ultimately crack us open to the awareness and experience of who we really are. Divine.

My challenges and life experiences were many. Starting with an unhappy childhood I have a memory of being trapped in a body and strapped in a high chair thinking – I have to get out of here. My parents were physically fighting with each other and I just wanted to get away from these people who lived in perpetual drama and suffering.

Who were they and why was I here? Who am I? These were the re-occurring questions in my mind.

Feeling misplaced and unhappy I grew into a joyless teenager who never smiled, hopelessness never left me. I attempted suicide a couple of times. This led me to realise that the professionals whom were counselling me were dysfunctional, unaware and just as unhappy as the rest of the world that I observed.

I was angry at life and saddened by it. This was my perspective. As it is with the ways of the universe, I stumbled across a book that gave me a reason for life. It introduced the concepts of reincarnation and taught that everyone has a purpose. I became aware that all that is experienced is designed for our spiritual growth and learning.

From that pivotal time I searched, read more books, trained and studied nutrition as well as many alternative therapies. My motivation and thirst for knowledge became even more important to me at the time of my first home birth to a divine being. I was so honoured and humbled that this baby chose me to facilitate his life.

I did not want to repeat what I had experienced as a child and even though it was not perfect I worked at providing the best start for this precious life.

My husband at that time was a highly evolved soul who taught me the benefits of meditation, spiritual philosophies and truths that gave me a greater understanding of and confronted the core of my ego.

As I continued to grow and find purpose in my life, it was seven years later that I had the privilege of another home birth. My life's circumstances at that time were challenging. My husband and I had separated and at five months of age my baby died of cot death. The pain was indescribable. Despite this we managed to re-unite our family and a year later I gave birth to a beautiful boy. During the birth I had a fleeting near death experience that awakened my heart to the most sublime light of bliss and peace.

Despite this enlightening experience, I was emotionally and mentally exhausted. The impact on me physically was undesirable.

Within, I knew that I had found my heart and began to surrender deeply. By letting go, this allowed me to open up even more and I started to feel a loving energy around me. It was the same energy that had shone so brightly in the near death state. Universal truths were felt within. I had a knowing that everything that had happened was part of a perfectly divine plan and meant to be.

After some time whilst teaching yoga, the most amazing phenomena were manifested by the channellings of the beings of light. The classes were full of healing energy, profound wisdom and joy. Many truths were revealed and taught. It was at this time that the ancient exercises came to me accompanied by a strange knowing from the depth of my soul that they had always been with me.

This is how the *Rites for Life* came to be. This daily ritual transformed me in ways that far exceeded my wildest dreams. I became physically stronger, more toned and vibrantly healthy. My emotions stabilised, my mind became focused and a wisdom flourished. My heart opened to an expansive joy and love that extended to all beings.

This heartfelt extension is a privilege and the opportunity to teach and facilitate the *Rites for Life* opens me ever more. To be witness to the countless transformations over 20 years is incredibly fulfilling and profoundly humbling.

It has been many years now and I continue to practise and teach this ritual and I am eternally grateful for the constant progression in life. They facilitate a healing regeneration, a mastery of energy and profound transformation, which allows one to become a beacon of light. Join us now to a joyful, healthful and purposeful life filled with the love that these magical Rites invoke. It is an honour to pass this knowledge to you and I whole-heartedly trust that you will shine brightly as a beautiful beacon - the light of truth for all humankind.

Namaste.

regenerate

The 5 Bodies 1 2 3 4 5

1 | THE PHYSICAL BODY

2 | THE EMOTIONAL BODY

3 | THE MENTAL BODY

4 | THE ENERGY BODY

5 | THE SPIRITUAL BODY

CLEARING THE
PHYSICAL, EMOTIONAL
& MENTAL BODIES

chapter 1
regenerate with energy

1 | THE PHYSICAL BODY

In part the *Rites for Life* are physical exercises similar to some yoga poses, yet the approach is subtly different. In traditional Hatha yoga for example the poses are static and the benefits are obtained by holding the poses for a length of time. With the *Rites for Life* practice you flow in and out of the poses, rather than holding them.

The breathing sequence is also very different to other types of yoga, and in some cases completely opposite to what you would usually do in a yoga class. This is because the *Rites for Life* are a tantric practice. Rather than focussing on the postures, muscles and the physical, the intention is on the inner energy body. The breath facilitates this, as energy is drawn up along the spine to naturally realign and balance the body. Working from within, shifts blockages and then the mind and body follows. This is an amazing and often very swift regeneration.

By working with energy like this I have witnessed people in mature years straighten their spine even some with kyphosis (a humped upper back) in a short period of time. Energy worked correctly aligns all aspects of being.

The physical body composes of various aspects and systems, including the muscles, bones, spine, internal organs, all systems of the hormones, digestive, circulatory, lymphatic, interconnecting with the organs such as the skin, liver, gallbladder, kidneys, intestines, stomach, elimination channels and essentially every cell of the body. Every cell of the body works individually and as a community to make the numerous systems work, heal and regenerate every millisecond. This is a natural process providing the conditions are favourable.

For the conditions to be in harmony, the body requires nothing to stand in its way to do the job nature intended. This is to heal. The human condition is often out of balance, which has a ripple effect to the cells of the body that make up our system. Many factors contribute to these imbalances and when we analyse the cause and try to understand why, we feed the energy of the condition.

What is required is to create the environment to allow the cells to function in perfection. From a physical point of view, the *Rites for Life* will do this as they help the cells to wake up and function as they should.

Stress inhibits the cells to function optimally, as do poor eating habits, dehydration, a lack of fresh air and exercise. Equally, the stress of dissatisfaction, lack of purpose and tumultuous relationships with family and work also impact the cells.

Breaking Habits

After teaching for many years and observing energy and the human condition I have come to realise that when we focus on getting rid of stress, when we desperately TRY to let it go, the opposite happens. That which we try to get rid of has a way of becoming larger than life, consuming us. The reason for this is we give our perceived problems more energy, allowing them to expand. If you are overweight for example, and you continually try to lose weight by saying I want to lose weight or I hate my fat, the cells of the body read the unintended message of 'fat' and that is what you get. This is the universal way of giving you what you place the most attention on. The universe does not discriminate. It has no concept of right, wrong, good or bad it just delivers what the focus is and your cells are transmitters and receivers of this.

There is another way of achieving enhanced health. Rather than trying and focusing on what you don't want, act on what gives you joy. This can be very tricky for it may give you joy having late nights, smoking and drinking alcohol. Regardless of what condition your mind and body are in, and what habits you choose, it is important not to judge and resist these habits. Accept them. Start with your *Rites for Life* practice and you will notice that harmful habits will naturally fall away. When your body is in harmony, it gravitates to more harmony. When you experience peace, you naturally attract more peace.

With experience the *Rites for Life* help people to engage and re-establish harmony. You naturally gravitate to drinking more water, eating fresh foods and engaging in healthy relationships. As you clear your energy centres day-by-day, the obstruction of unhealthy habits does not control you, it has lost its charge, its craving, its destructiveness. Unhelpful habits lose their power. No matter where you are in your life, give attention and energy to perfect health and the cells will follow your instruction. You are the master and your cells are your honouring servants. Master them lovingly and reward them with natures goodness and they in turn will serve all the systems of the body.

The physical benefits of the *Rites for Life* are many and include:

- *Strengthens and tones the muscles*
- *Increases flexibility*
- *Massages internal organs*
- *Balances hormones*
- *Improves overall appearance, skin tone, brighter eyes, fuller face*
- *Greater endurance*
- *Enhances all other physical activities*
- *Greater energy levels*
- *Alignment of spine*
- *Improves digestion and elimination*
- *Encourages healthier choices in eating habits*
- *Less desire for overindulgence of food and drink*
- *Regeneration on a cellular level*
- *Further oxygenation, more supply of universal life force*
- *Stimulates greater healing capacity of injuries and wounds*

Practising the *Rites for Life* daily helps you to release conditioning that leads to degeneration without force or trying. The rebalancing and re-programming occurs effortlessly.

2 | THE EMOTIONAL BODY

The body, emotions, mind and spirit are interlinked. That which is experienced through the emotions ripples through all the other bodies. The emotional body can appear very complex if analysed. As explained, what you give attention and energy to expands and grows. The universal force does not discriminate between good, bad, right or wrong it only delivers without judgment that which is focused upon. The emotions can rule our lives and create a fluctuating range of experiences - joyful, sad, angry, happy, depressed and many more.

Clearing this emotional roller-coaster ride requires an understanding that emotions are energy and the nature of energy is that it comes and goes. Analysis of the emotions and the associated stories can create a mountain out of a molehill. Allowing emotional energy to flow requires awareness that you are not the emotion; you are not the experience. You are the one observing the experience. The observer is the real you and it does not have opinion, analysis or attachment. Let go of wanting to know. Attachment to wanting anything creates blockage. If you want you can't have, because you are continually in a state of wanting and not having.

To have requires you to simply be. Vibrate at that level of already having, and then it will come. When we are vibrating at a higher level, we naturally attract what is for our highest good, what is meant to be, and there is a peace in that. Surrender the details to the universe and allow your emotions to be a tool for expression and peace rather than confusion and chaos.

We can observe that when a stressed thought arises for example and if it continues to persist, it eventually expresses itself through the emotional body often as an emotional outburst as a way of releasing. Remember the thought is energy and the nature of energy requires a flow, in and out, experienced and released. If the emotional volatility is not expressed and released, it eventually transpires to the physical body manifesting as illness and even disease.

I remember one time when my son was in his early teens and being completely obnoxious and resistant to any assistance that was offered to him. This went on and on and on and I tried harder and harder to be very patient. Yet, trying to be patient did not work. One day I had to walk away and yelled out in frustration - "I hate this, I hate this, I hate this." Thankfully, I had enough insight not to feel guilty about being so angry. I realised then that I had admitted honestly the thought that I was working so hard at resisting and all I needed to do without judgment and analysis was accept and be aware of the way that I felt.

Strangely enough my beautiful son started to be more co-operative. For me this was powerfully affirmative. If we allow ourselves to embrace emotions fully, accept them, they then very naturally go away. Since that time I have never felt the intensity of those emotions again.

Dispassionately embrace the emotion without judgment, acknowledge it without suppression and remember it is just energy wanting to be released. So how do we do this easily? By moving the body - walking, running, dancing, yoga or the *Rites for Life* will shift the emotional state and prevent blockage. Many people that practise the *Rites for Life* report that these tools dramatically help in releasing feelings that inhibit joy and love of life. The experience is one of 'oh! that feels better not sure why or how, yet what a relief!'

It is essential not to be attached to the how and why. Most often it is a reaction to an experience of the past, which has stored in the sub-conscious mind ready to be embraced and set free. It does not matter where it came from or the circumstances. This is irrelevant to your spiritual growth and paying attention to it only ensures it goes round and round, getting larger and larger. If understanding is required for your spiritual growth you are more likely to have clarity once you let it go. Clearing disturbances from the emotional body is essential for abundant health and well-being.

Benefits of clearing the body emotional include:

- *Greater capacity for joy and expression*
- *Ability to let go of past hurts*
- *Stress relief*
- *Expands the heart centre*
- *Positive ripple effect for the mind and body*
- *Greater ease in relationship with others*
- *Achievement of emotional equilibrium*
- *Consistent and stable*

When practising the Rites we are clearing and regenerating the emotions. This enables us to experience a greater love and joy of life.

3 | THE MENTAL BODY

"A busy mind is a stressed mind, a quiet mind is sound, and a still mind is Divine".

The mental body is closely linked to the emotional body, which then affects the physical body. The *Rites for Life* includes, as part of the practice, a meditation technique that helps clear the mind of accumulated stressful mental chatter. In meditation it is the stillness even for only a few moments that allows one to tap into the Universal mind, an expansive awareness, a knowing that in truth cannot be described yet can be experienced. Once experienced if only for a few moments with continued practise the experience expands.

Meditation brings one closer to the reality of the Self, the Divine, and an awareness that transcribes into day-to-day life. Living from the inside out changes our perspective on life for greater peace and clarity. We become aware of the choices that we make, what we create, awareness that we are ultimately all One. We take full responsibility for all actions and reactions in life and have an uncompromising knowing of the Illusion, the Game of Life. We have a greater capacity to let go and not take life too seriously for it is a Game, a wonderful game that we have chosen to play. Why not play the game wisely, for surely we are here to enlighten to who we are?

We surrender to the real Self and know that in life whatever is presented to us is of our own energetic creation and therefore to be dealt with joyously. Awareness deals with circumstances in non-reaction and peace, awareness does not judge or analyse, awareness is universal consciousness that encompasses complete unconditional love. This expansive, all embracing divinity is within. To seek for it in the game, the illusion, will only lead to dissatisfaction, frustration and suffering.

Meditation cleanses the mental body. A clear mind does not hold onto energies that as stated before need to be released. In meditation as a thought arises and when the attitude of non-attachment is practised the thought passes like a cloud in the sky.

Many thoughts arise in meditation and with continued practise of allowing the thoughts to come and go our mind empties of all transitory concepts. When no concepts attach then we are in touch with the universal mind, the all-pervasive, omnipotent, omnipresent divinity of being.

Imagine if you could feel, live and be this way. You may choose to work towards it, you may choose to be it now, you may choose not to. It is always your choice. You may choose to practise the *Rites for Life*, which serve as a preparation for the meditation. Thus, helping you to surrender, remember your chosen path and to become more aware.

Benefits of clearing the mind:

- *Clarity of purpose*
- *Peace and joy*
- *Increased awareness*
- *Enhanced intelligence*
- *Greater ability for decision-making*
- *Improved concentration*
- *Ability to be present*
- *Better sleep*
- *More focused*

Choose to practise the *Rites for Life* meditation, a profoundly healing and releasing way to joy!

4 | THE ENERGY BODY

We are made of universal energy and it is within all that is manifested from the smallest insect to human beings. Universal energy is in the concrete and grass, it is everything that is seen, felt, heard, tasted and smelt. The things that are closer to nature have more life force. For example the grass has a greater supply of energy compared to concrete. The more aware and closer to our natural state we are, the greater our ability to tap into this universal life force.

If you experience feelings of tiredness, it is usually a result of being disconnected from the life force energy. Tapping into the energy body through practise can be done any time of the day simply by taking a deep expansive inhalation, keeping the shoulders down and relaxed, connecting to your inner energy body. Exhale through the nose, and then your next in breath will have more prana. If you have times when you only have a few hours sleep, pay extra attention to your breathing, taking deeper and slower breaths. Particularly when you are doing your *Rites for Life* the breath will give you an abundance of energy. Even when you are not doing the *Rites for Life* and your energy levels are fading throughout the day, stop and take a few energetic breaths in and out of the nose to refuel your energy tank.

Correct breathing encourages a greater supply of prana, as the Yogis have known for thousands of years. This universal life force is in every cell of your body and when an abundance of it is present the cells become enlivened and function at an optimum level. Cells that are infused with greater energy levels can then regenerate and heal the body. The natural healing process is not possible without a free flowing supply of energy. A blocked energy field has less prana, less life force.

When an abundance of prana is present in a person, you sense it, their energy is expansive, and they are full of light and exude a healing presence. Equally an abundance of prana is present in the ocean, mountains, forests and many places on this earth have this healing power.

Awareness of the energy in nature helps us to connect with and appreciate taking a walk in nature, the beauty of the trees, animals, oceans, mountains and forests.

Observing the magic of nature cultivates an openness of heart, a peace of mind, a knowing that this perfection is a reflection of you. Wherever we place our attention the universal healing energy will follow.

Benefits for clearing the energy body with the *Rites for Life* include:

- *A mastery of directing energy to all parts of the body for healing*
- *The ability to tap into the universal life force or prana for greater energy*
- *Helps to experience greater physical and mental energy*
- *Opening and expanding the specific energy centres called the chakras*

5 | THE SPIRITUAL BODY

The *Rites for Life* are an energetic tantric practice. They are an ancient system that enlivens, expands and regenerates our main energy fields. The Rites activate a universal life force that cleanses these energy aspects of our being, creating an unobstructed path to the spiritual. As these blockages clear an expansive awareness is experienced.

The spiritual is an expanded consciousness; it encompasses all the previous bodies, yet does not translate as a thought, feeling or sensation. It is the state of a pure awareness of oneness. No mind created concepts reside.

We are multi-dimensional beings and when energy flows a consciousness reveals itself. You find your true nature. The light within you can shine and the light of awareness, which was always there presents.

How do you experience the spiritual body?

It can be experienced in deep meditation once the other three bodies are cleared through the practise of the Rites.

6 | CLEARING THE PHYSICAL, EMOTIONAL & MENTAL BODIES

As part of teaching and facilitating the *Rites for Life* workshops – a channelled visualisation was included. This helped participants get a highly effective kick-start to their growth and healing. The clearer the energy bodies the more profoundly effective your Rites practice will be.

As human being we have many energy sheaths that are connected and extend to the universal all. Beyond the mental, emotional and physical bodies we have several spiritual bodies or energy sheaths of higher vibratory rates. To experience an unobstructed flow to these higher spiritual sheaths the lower three bodies require clearing. The *Rites for Life* exercises cleanse these bodies and further enhance this free flow of energy to higher vibratory energies, an unobstructed path to the divine. This healing and clearing practice greatly assists your spiritual evolvement.

You may practise this technique lying down or sitting in an upright position, in a meditation pose or on a chair. Whether you are lying down or sitting it is required that your body is aligned and that you are deeply relaxed without interruption.

Once in your preferred relaxed position, take a few deep breaths in through the nose and release a sound of Hahh through the mouth. Throughout the practice continue breathing effortlessly in and out of the nose.

Ask for help

Now allow yourself to direct your awareness to your heart centre and ask for help from the universal force. Asking for help is done in innocence, without expectation and not being concerned with whom you are asking. This universal force is healing and ultimately is not separate from you or all that exists. By asking for help you are inviting the divine consciousness of your inner self, which is the universe to heal and clear the lower bodies for greater clarity and awareness.

White light

Begin by imagining or seeing in your minds eye a brilliant white universal light that descends from the heavens of the universe that will help you clear these three bodies.

Clearing the mental body

We will start with becoming aware of the mental body or sheath, which extends several feet or metres beyond the body yet connected to it. The mental body consists of all your thought forms and also holds thought forms of all mass thoughts of the inhabitants of the Earth. We are all connected and mass planetary conscious thought forms influence your own personal mental body, which also influences the mass.

These thought forms are not who you are. Thought forms consist of concepts that the mind is often overloaded with. They have no truth. For example, religious, economical, psychological concepts. The sense that you are separate from, notions of right and wrong, good and bad, are all conditioned societal beliefs. These thought forms are conceptual constructs that pollute the mental body.

To clear the mental body begin by seeing or imagining a brilliant white light descending from above your head; direct this clearing and healing energy to flow into the crown of the head and allow it to flow along the spine, piercing through the chakras as it moves through the centre of the body down to the base of the spine, the base chakra and then flowing down into the toes.

As this light flows down, it is breaking up the mental body debris and softening stuck mental constructs.

When this light reaches your toes; slowly redirect it up along the centre of the body and allow it to flow; gathering with it all of the mental concepts that no longer serve you.

Keep visualising this light moving up and then releasing out of the crown of your head. Allow the mental debris that you are ready to let go of transcend beyond the mental body and for the universe to burn out and transmute it.

All that has no truth by way of the universal law will no longer exist once it has been released to the higher dimensional realms.

Complete this process one more time to effectively clear the mental body. Do not be attached to what you are letting go of and be aware not to use the mind, to clear the mind. This is like trying to clear one concept with another one. Serving only to add to the mental over activity. Place your trust in the light and know that it is doing the work for you. Surrender to its help.

You have now cleared and cleansed mental body. Become aware of the clarity of mind, the freedom from confusion. Bathe in this spaciousness and know that this spaciousness is pure consciousness.

Clearing the emotional body

Direct your attention and the healing white light to the emotional body, where all your emotions reside.

This energy sheath is a few metres below the mental body and a few metres beyond the physical energy body. It is where you hold and store all emotions and reactions to life. This body is also affected by the feelings of the mass consciousness. Some refer to this body or energy sheath as the lower astral field. When this body is burdened by emotions, they stand in the way of the true expression and experience of unconditional love and joy.

Emotions such as fear, anger, frustration, sadness and many more result in overloading this energy field. This overload stands in the way of you expressing your birth right of joy, love and peace.

Allow and direct this brilliant light of healing to flow from the heavens into the crown of the head of the emotional body. Feel it flow down the centre of the body piercing the chakras and spreading to every part of the emotional body - softening and breaking up all the emotions that are ready to be released.

Feel the light flow down to the toes and then redirect this light up along the spine as it gathers all the emotional debris.

Do this slowly and feel the clearing up along the body and up out of the crown of the head to be burnt and transmuted by the higher vibrational energies.

Repeat this process one more time, slowly, with an effortless focus on thoroughly cleansing the emotional body. Know the energy of the beautiful white light is there to help you.

Without attachment, take the time to observe the emotions that do not serve you and realise that they were not and are not who you really are. Feel the deep sense of joy and love that you have inside of you. It has always been there and now that you have cleared this body you can express the beauty of this love and joy in your day-to-day life. Take the time to bathe in its bliss. Be at peace and enjoy your being.

Clearing the physical body

Now direct your awareness and this brilliant white light to the physical body. Every cell, muscle, tissue, bone, all systems of the physical body are going to be bathed and permeated in healing light. Allow this light to flow into the crown of the head and deeply penetrating on an atomic and cellular level down through the body, firstly filling the whole of the head, brain, face and neck with light.

Feel it filling your shoulders and both your arms and hands with healing loving light, going down to the whole of the back and spine and now spreading light to the whole of your torso and permeating the internal organs and every digestive eliminatory channel of the body. All systems of the physical bathed in light, healing and regenerating each and every cell.

Direct it now and let it flow to your hips and buttocks down along your legs to your feet and toes. Your whole body is filled with the light of healing and rejuvenation, feel it and be it. You are filled with light, allow yourself to expand this light of healing by staying effortlessly present for a few moments.

The longer you hold your awareness with the light the more profoundly healing it is. Then bring your attention to this universal light and direct it upward along the whole of the body and all systems of the body. Travelling upward and out. This universal light castes out all that is not of the light of the physical body and releases out the crown of the head. All impurities and toxins flowing out and to be burned and transmuted.

You are regenerating, you have an energy of perfect health and harmony, embrace this, this is you without the impurities. You are one with the light. So be it, it is done.

You have cleared and cleansed these three major energy bodies, which now allow you a deeper more profound connection to the divine.

Slowly start to take some deeper breaths and breathe in through the nose and release with a big releasing sigh out of the mouth. Give yourself a deep long stretch, raising your arms overhead and tighten every muscle of the body for a few moments then release, relax and let go for another few moments.

Finish this practice by standing up and bouncing on your heels, keeping the knees soft. Shimmer and shake your body so as to ground the energies to the here and now. Do this for a minute, then place your hands in prayer position to your heart and express a heart-felt gratitude firstly to yourself and thank the universe for its divine help.

To understand how this universal energy affects us, the next chapter will describe the chakras, our inner energy centres.

The 7 chakras

7 | CROWN CHAKRA

6 | THIRD EYE CHAKRA

5 | THROAT CHAKRA

4 | HEART CHAKRA

3 | SOLAR PLEXUS CHAKRA

2 | SACRAL SEXUAL CHAKRA

1 | ROOT BASE CHAKRA

chapter 2
healing your chakras

Learning about the human energy system is a means to self-understanding, self-discovery and gives you a greater awareness of your personal strengths and weaknesses. Chakras are a very important part of this system and the understanding of the esoteric science behind the Rites. The awareness of these subtle yet powerful energy centres is crucial for your health and spiritual growth.

A chakra is a spinning vortex of energy created within the body. The word chakra comes from the Sanskrit word for 'wheel' or 'disk' and originated within the philosophy of the ancient Yoga system of India and Tibet. Centuries ago, the Yoga masters realised that the human being consisted of more than just the physical body; they believed that the physical, mental, emotional and spiritual aspects of the individual were inter-related. The masters also believed that the spinning vortexes of energy overlap and correspond to various physical organs and glands and that these chakras can be regulated and harmonised, resulting in the unleashing of an individuals full potential of health, happiness and spiritual awareness.

There are seven major chakras arranged vertically along the spine, starting at the base of the spine and ending at the crown of the head. While the chakras do exist within the physical body, exhibiting a strong influence on such aspects as body shape or health, they are not made of any physical components themselves. For instance, a physician could not operate on a chakra any more than on an emotion, yet both can, and do affect us physically.

The chakras correspond to major areas of your life, such as survival, sex, power, love, communication, perception and understanding. To use a practical analogy, the chakras can be seen as your internal software that stores your programming about how to function in life. The base chakra, for instance, contains your survival program, such as what and when you eat, and when you need to sleep, exercise and protect yourself.

Your body is the computer hardware, and each of us has a slightly different model, programmed in a distinct language, with unique operating systems. Ideally, we can work with chakras, to examine the programming without judgment and self criticism - observe the destructive programming without attachment and consciously, in awareness, let go or delete all the programming that does not serve us well.

Chakras also correspond to the elements of earth, water, fire, air, ether (space), with a level of consciousness, with a sense and with a dimension. Numerous other elements, such as colour, sounds, herbs, crystals and mantras have also been correlated to the chakras and are sometimes used as tools for accessing and developing these energy centres.

Chakras are often referred to as lotuses, for they open and close like a flower and, in Tantric Yoga, they are shown with a varying number of petals. The petals range from four at the base chakra to one thousand or more at the crown.

When a chakra is closed, the life force energy or prana cannot travel through that part of the body. If this is the case, you may feel a lack in your life in its related area; for example, the throat chakra relates to communication. Therefore if it is blocked or closed, communication is difficult and, on the physical side of health, a blocked chakra may manifest itself as a sore throat or tight neck.

A chakra can also be overblown if it is out of balance. In this case, that particular chakra uses so much of the body's energy and the mind's attention, that other areas become deficient. For instance, an overblown third chakra (the solar plexus, which relates to our personal power) may cause an attachment to holding power over others and possibly depleting the heart chakra.

Developing your chakras

With awareness and understanding you can open and expand your chakras. They can be developed like muscles, programmed like a computer; nurtured like a seed or closed like a book. Development of the chakras occurs through working on specific areas. There are varying techniques taught to balance, cleanse and open the chakras. The *Rites for Life* are the most effective method.

To experience what a chakra feels like, try the following exercise. Sit comfortably with your arms straight out in front of you, elbows straight. Turn one palm downward and one palm up. Quickly, with repeated motions, open and close your fists tightly as fast and as long as you can. Switch the positions of your palms and repeat until your hands are tired. Drop your arms, open your fists and bring your palms together slowly, moving them together and out again.

Do you feel a ball of energy between your hands? If you tune in closely, you can feel the spinning. These are your hand chakras, a smaller version of your seven major spinal chakras.

We are currently in the Aquarian Age, which is an age of awareness. It's as if we are being pulled along with great speed to address and cleanse all aspects of our physical, emotional, mental and spiritual beings. Most of us have been trained to rely primarily on our brain power for information.

By tuning into the consciousness received through the body by the chakras, we will be more in tune with higher mental and spiritual energies and freer from restrictive brain programming allowing us to live with less suffering and more joy.

To understand how to access your chakras, it is necessary to understand the concept of prana (sometimes referred to as Chi or Ki), which means life force. prana is the essence of all motion, force or energy and is manifested in gravitation, electricity and all forms of life. We are constantly inhaling air charged with prana and extracting prana from the air for the body to use for its various functions. When we breathe, we absorb and extract sufficient prana for the normal body functions. Conscious breathing exercises or pranayama, allows us to extract a greater supply of prana.

This prana is stored away in the nerve centres, producing vitality and a reserve of this energy is used and can be directed to the chakras and the associated glands and organs for healing and regeneration.

The chakras are interconnected so that prana can flow to every part of the body along many channels called nadis. At the point where nadis intersect, chakras are formed. The nadis are non-physical energy channels that are the same channels acupuncturists work on, although acupuncturists call them meridians.

Serpent Goddess

According to Tantric Yoga, the chakras are used as focal points in space to draw in the cosmic energy at the vital life centres with visualisation, meditation and breath control (pranayama). When a tantric practitioner awakens the Kundalini they will feel the energy travelling up the major chakras.

Kundalini is a concept often spoken of in relation to the chakras. Mythologically, kundalini is a serpent Goddess who lies asleep at the base of the spine, coiled three and a half times around the base chakra, awaiting unfoldment. When she is awakened through any of a number of techniques, she unfolds and rises through the shusumna channel, piercing and awakening each chakra as she goes. When she has risen to the crown chakra, then all chakras have been opened and a person is said to experience enlightenment.

Kundalini is a strong and powerful force that can produce radical mental and physical changes. The Rites prepare and cleanse the chakras so that the kundalini energy can flow through the spine without obstruction. It can be an awakening experience but it is generally not advisable to invoke kundalini without an experienced teacher who will help and guide you through the changes. It is, however, a profound healing force and a powerfully effective way to connect with the universe.

1 | MULADHARA CHAKRA - Root Base Centre

The first chakra is located at the base of the spine, tip of the coccyx and the point you are sitting on right now. It is the seat of your 'drive'. Muladhara means 'root' and the paths of energy in this chakra extend downward like a root through the legs and feet to contact the solid earth below.

A simple way to energise this chakra is to sit up straight in your chair with your feet flat against the floor and push slightly into your feet. Your legs will tighten a bit and there will be an increased flow into your base chakra. As you relax your legs and feet, you will feel the flow recede and, as you tighten them, you can feel your body becoming more solid. This is a simple way you can increase the flow of energy into your lower body.

The element associated with the first chakra is earth. Earth is solid and heavy, earth is below us and earth supplies us with our survival needs: food, clothing and shelter. The universal force that flows downward like roots, toward the earth is gravity. The force of gravity allows us to stay connected with the Earth. When we allow ourselves to flow gracefully with gravity, we are in harmony with the downward flow of the first chakra. The common term for this flow as it occurs in the human body is 'grounding'. Grounding is a process of dynamic contact with the Earth that occurs through our feet and legs. When grounding is done appropriately our whole body is nourished and energised and we feel the healing earth's energies.

Eating is a basic first chakra survival activity. Without food, we do not survive very long. Eating disorders (too much or too little) often indicate first chakra imbalance. Eating is a grounding activity - it helps us to feel settled, calm and secure. Excess weight can be an attempt to ground out high stress, to protect the body or emotions. Eating too little or being chronically underweight can be an attempt to avoid grounding and physicality because it seems too frightening or confronting.

The six chakras that correspond to the physical body have a companion chakra. The base chakra's companion is the heart chakra. These two chakras have a direct relationship, for instance if the base chakra is out of balance, the driving force of the base chakra could not awaken the opening of the heart centre.

2 | SVADHISTHANA CHAKRA - Sacral Sexual Centre

The second chakra is in the lower abdomen centred just below the navel. It corresponds to the sacral vertebrae and the nerve ganglion called the sacral plexus. It is the seat of our creativity. The Sanskrit name means 'sweetness'. Its element is water. Therefore the chakra corresponds with bodily functions that have to do with liquid: circulation, urinary elimination, sexuality and reproduction.

The seat of creativity manifests in many ways and underlies many activities. Our sexual energy underlies every act of individual expression. It is a creative force - the influence of which extends far beyond sexual activity to include thought, feelings, behaviour and this energy can even influence art, music, fashion and many other manifestations of creativity. This centre is highly active and its energy permeates virtually everything we do. It is vitally fundamental to both basic creativity and higher ecstasy.

If this chakra is too open, there is a tendency to feel everyone else's emotions or to be overly ruled by your emotions with frequent and dramatic emotional episodes. If the chakra is closed down, then we are flat, dull, and lifeless. We are out of touch with our emotions and have very little desire or passion and little or no interest in sexuality.

Svadhisthana Chakra has a direct link to the throat chakra. For instance if the sex centre is out of balance one can usually detect this in a person's tone of voice. If the voice is high and shrill or unusually deep for a woman this is an indicator that the sexual centre is closed down.

3 | MANIPURA CHAKRA - Solar Plexus

The third chakra is located at the solar plexus. It is the centre of the individual self and the seat of power. Its name means 'lustrous gem', we can think of it as a glowing yellow sun radiating through the centre of our body. Its element is fire - fire that radiates and transforms matter into energy, giving light and warmth. Digestive troubles, ulcer or addictions to stimulants are all related to malfunctioning of this chakra.

When the third chakra is closed down one may feel tired, shaky, quiet or withdrawn. There is a fear of taking risks, confronting people or issues, taking charge and a lack of energy. If the chakra is too open, then we have a kind of bully archetype, someone who needs to be in control, to dominate, to seek power, prestige and ambition.

This chakra generates the drive towards self-assertion, personal determination and individual strength, preparing us to meet the challenges of the living world. This centre is enormously powerful and is also associated with 'gut' intuition and personal charisma. A good way for stimulating the third chakra is to get your energy moving by doing your Rites, releasing stuck energies in this chakra.

Manipura chakra's companion is the third eye centre. The 'gut' feelings we sometimes experience as basic instinctual knowing are related to the third eye's inner spiritual awareness.

4 | ANAHATA CHAKRA - Heart Centre

The fourth chakra lies at the point of the spine across from the sternum at the centre of the chest. It is the seat of the 'higher self'. We are now halfway through our seven-leveled chakra system. Lying midway between the lower three and higher three chakras, the fourth centre marks the point of conscious departure from lower to higher awareness.

The heart chakra is related to the element air and the quality of unconditional love. Air is formless, largely invisible, expansive, as it will expand to fit any space, yet it is soft and gentle. So too is pure love. Love is the expansion of the heart, the transcendence of boundaries, the inter-connectedness of your spirit or higher self.

If the heart centre is closed down, the very core of us suffers. Our breathing is shallow; slowing down our metabolism and our physical energy; we also tend to withdraw and become a closed system. When the heart chakra is too open, there is a tendency to give all our time and energy away, to be so focused on 'other' that we lose our own centre.

Ideally the heart should radiate love from a strong, solid centre of self-acceptance and reach out with supportive care and compassion towards others. The operating force in this chakra is the force of equilibrium. That which stays in balance has longevity and lives in joy and harmony. Allow yourself to be in touch with the peaceful loving balance of the heart within yourself and with others and experience the abundance of universal love and healing.

To balance this expansive centre, primarily all you need is to expand your chest, have a good posture, breathe the life force or prana into your heart and feel one with the universe.

5 | VISUDDHA CHAKRA - Throat Centre

The fifth chakra is located at the spine directly behind the centre of the throat. It is the seat of 'concepts', how we perceive concepts and communicate them. The element associated with this level is ether or 'akasha' meaning spirit, as well as the element of sound. From sound we get communication. Communication is the activity and function of this fifth chakra. Through this chakra flow the energies for the higher functions of communication and personal expression.

Communication involves both listening and speaking. If your throat chakra is closed down then there is a fear of expressing yourself, fear of speaking your truth, or excessive shyness. If the chakra is too open, you are so busy expressing that you forget to listen and be present.

Ideally the throat chakra should be connected to self and to be a strong self-expressive vehicle of truth, which has a growing awareness of the many concepts that cloud our truth.

6 | AJNA CHAKRA - Third Eye

The sixth chakra resides between the eyebrows and inward toward the centre of the head. The third eye is the seat of insight and inner vision directed by wisdom and a deep understanding of the subtle forces at play in any given situation. Its name Ajna means to 'perceive'.

Those who are open on this level are confident to trust their intuition. If the third eye is too open you can have an unbalanced perspective of spiritual energies and auras. If the chakra is closed down without solid ground to back it up, one may experience hallucinations, confusion from too much input, or over interpretation of everyday occurrences. A good exercise to develop the visualisation capacity of the third eye, while simultaneously helping to balance all your chakras, is to focus on each one of your chakras in a meditative state.

7 | SAHASRARA CHAKRA - Crown Centre

Located above the crown of the head, the seventh chakra is the centre of spiritual consciousness. It is a state of absolute awareness. It is an unconditional state of total fulfillment, the embodiment of total freedom, wisdom, energy, insight and joy.

At this level, you realise unity with all manifestations of the universe. You are at the centre of the universe and the concept of separateness does not exist. This finding of the true self corresponds to the transmutation of energies from the lower chakras to the crown, thus experiencing an 'oneness' or illumination.

Chakra visualisation

After you have completed your Rites it's recommended that you take time to relax to fully assimilate all the exercise. I teach a colour healing meditation that takes about half an hour to practise, though you should feel free to meditate longer. You can include the visualisation after you complete your Rites for the relaxation. You can either seat yourself cross-legged comfortably on the floor or if you require spinal support sit with your back straight up against the back of a chair. Place your hands on your knees. Eyes and mouth gently closed, with the tip of your tongue touching the upper palate. In this position breathe steadily and easily in and out of the nose for several minutes. As you do this release any tension in your muscles except for what you need to sit straight. Allow your shoulders, abdomen and facial muscles to become totally relaxed.

Now allow yourself to surrender your will and desires, your fears and anxieties and all that does not serve you to the loving healing energies of the universe. From deep within your heart with strength, power and sincerity ask for help from the universe.

Healing white light

Now visualise a brilliant healing white light to surround the whole of your body, for love, healing and protection. This beaming light will follow your mind's attention as you work through your chakras. Throughout this healing visualisation breathing is vitally important. So breathe slightly deeper than normal, steadily, evenly and relaxed. Maintain this breathing throughout this visualisation.

Aura

Now bring your attention to the space all around your body, the aura. The aura is an energetic sheath that extends from the body in all directions. Focus your attention on that energetic sheath, extending outward from the body for at least a foot or more. With every breath, feel as though the aura is becoming increasingly concentrated with energy. As much as possible really feel that space all around you.

After you have brought your attention up through the chakras and to the aura, sit quietly, breathing slowly and steadily, allowing your entire system to assimilate the energy flow. Let your mind be still and quiet. Expect nothing and do not try to provoke any particular experience. Instead, be aware of the moment; really be here now. Be aware of your body posture, of the breath flowing in and out, of the feeling of the air around you, of the sights and smells of your surroundings. Conclude your practise in this state of attention. Taking time to be still at the end of the physical practice to allow the energy that you have released to flow through and place the attention to the crown chakra. Energy when surrendered releases out the top of the head. Now take a few deep breaths, rub your hands together vigorously, and then slowly rub them over your face. Open your eyes and relax a moment or two before becoming more active.

1ST CHAKRA

Now direct your attention to the first chakra, Muladhara, at the tip of the coccyx. Focus your attention here, direct the healing white light to balance and cleanse this chakra, working on all levels - emotional, mental and physical. Now visualise the most brilliant fiery red colour at the base of the spine and keep your attention here for about three minutes or so while breathing slowly and steadily. With every breath, you are breathing the healing life force into the very centre of that chakra. Really feel this place in your body and allow it to be fully relaxed.

2ND CHAKRA

From Muladhara, move your attention and awareness to the second chakra, Svadhisthana, located at the lower spine at the level of the sex organs. Focus your attention here for a few minutes while directing the healing white light to work with you. Now visualise a pure orange colour permeating this area while you are breathing slowly and steadily, again with each breath, feel as though you are breathing right through this centre of energy. Really feel this place in your body.

3RD CHAKRA

The next point of attention is the third chakra, Manipura located along the spine at the area of the solar plexus. Direct the healing white light to this area and breathe slowly and steadily for a few minutes. Now visualise a brilliant sun-gold yellow colour permeating this area with warmth. As much as possible feel this centre, healing and balancing with every breath.

4TH CHAKRA

Focus next on the fourth chakra, Anahata located at the spine directly opposite the chest just below the breastbone. Bring all your awareness here for three minutes or so and direct this universal healing, loving white light to your heart centre. Now visualise a beautiful apple green colour permeating this area, breathing slowly and steadily. With every breath feel your heart expanding and once again from deep within this centre ask for help. Feel the healing and love penetrating deep into your heart, stay focused and feel this as much as possible.

5TH CHAKRA

Bring your strength to the fifth chakra, Visuddha located at the spine across from the centre of the throat. Focus your attention here for a few minutes and once again direct the white light to this area. Feel the cleansing and balancing energy of the healing white light and now visualise a blue, the most glorious blue - a little darker than the sky blue colour. Feel this blue permeate your throat centre and really feel this centre as you continue to breathe deeply and steadily.

6TH CHAKRA

Your awareness and this brilliant white light are focused on the third eye centre, Ajna, the spot between the eyebrows. Focus your attention here for three minutes or so and visualise an indigo colour permeating your third eye. With every breath feel this centre beaming with spiritual intuition. As much as possible, really feel and stay focused on this area.

7TH CHAKRA

From the third eye bring your attention to the crown chakra, Sahasrana, at the top of the head. Focus your awareness here for three minutes or so and direct the universal healing white light, two or three inches above the crown of your head. As much as possible, feel the entire top of your head ablaze with this healing energy.

master energy

chapter 3
the power of I am

WANTING & HAVING

Your life can be a series of choices between wanting and having. It can be equated to an on and off switch. The wanting choice is the off switch and the having is the on switch. The wanting switch has an unseen, unspoken universal message on it. Wanting is the sum total of all your wanting, with this you unknowingly create a lack of money, a lack in a particular part of the body or lack in a particular relationship. Wanting includes both your aversions and attachments to having something happen in a certain way. The message is lack. You must choose and know you cannot have and want at the same time. It is like you cannot both stand up and sit down simultaneously.

If you choose the on switch (the having), then you receive this unseen energetic message of freedom from wanting. It is only then that you can have all that is meant to be for you in life. Your energy raises, you turn the light on and move from darkness. Courage, acceptance and peace are the higher energies that come when you choose the on switch.

If you are not achieving your goals in life, you are leaving your switches set on the off switch of wanting. There is no wanting if you show up fully and choose freedom over everything else. Choose the on switch of having, for it is the switch of freedom. The truth will be revealed that you have already, always had, always will. Now watch as your life falls into alignment and don't be surprised when your inner heart have's come to be. This is a play with words that your subconscious mind your computer program relates to. From a universal perspective it is the 'I am'.

RITES FOR LIFE - 'I AM' - AFFIRMING STATEMENTS

Keeping your attention focused on the practice is not always easy. It's natural for your mind to wander to external concerns and demands. 'I am' statements have been introduced to prevent the mind from wandering and connect you to the energy of each Rite.

For example when you start spinning, you are connecting to the energy of light. By affirming "I am light" expands the light energy exponentially. It also connects the energy of light with the mind, the subconscious and the conscious.

On a spiritual level it evokes a remembering of that which you already are and brings you fully into the present. This is felt on all levels of your being. On a mental level you are present. Emotionally you experience the energy. Physically you become light. The 'I am' statement, which has been used for centuries by the Yogis, confirms the truth of the omnipresence and omnipotence of that which is within. Affirming 'I am' and any statement made following has a powerful vibration that reverberates on a deep cellular level.

In the self-help industry positive affirmations are used to shift the mind from self-depreciating thoughts to positive ones in order to shift the consciousness to higher vibration states of peace, abundance and happiness. The 'I am' statement is the most effective. It is a statement made in the present affirming that which you already are. Some may think it to be presumptuous but why not assume you are all that is magnificent. With each Rite the 'I am' statement is designed to encourage the transformational energy of that affirmation to manifest in the here and now.

If any one of these statements makes you uncomfortable you may have discovered a very important resistance. This is a positive awareness. The resistance often is a result of family conditioning and programming.

Generally speaking many people were told that they needed to obtain to become better, not to be selfish and so on. It can be very confronting to use these affirming statements for it is almost the exact opposite to your conditioning. The I am statements are another way of reprogramming and letting go of old conditioning that does not serve.

The way to deal with resistance is to simply accept that you have it. It may be helpful to say 'Yes to resistance', and not judge yourself for the resistance. Resistance is an indicator of what we need to let go of. You may be comfortable with some statements and not with others, and be aware that our greater resistance or fear is our greatest strength. Remember you are working with the tools that weaken resistance. Awareness and acceptance to any emotion releases the energy that often controls us and stands in the way of moving forward.

Do the exercises and after a while you may find that with increased awareness that the *Rites for Life* will assist you to connect to the universal truth of these statements. Most importantly always remember to work at your own level and within your comfort zone. You do progress and grow with a dedication to the practice on whatever level you choose.

The affirming statements are to be chanted in time with the breath and movement to ensure a focused mind. To practise, breathe in holding the pose for two seconds and make the statement out loud or within, and then release the breath and the position, ready to repeat.

THE IMPLEMENTATION OF THE 'I AM' STATEMENTS

The affirming statements for each Rite are designed to enhance your healing and awareness. It is vitally important to experience the intended energy and really feel it.

Please be aware that with practise the 'I am' statements will help you to connect with these universal truths and in your own time, will become part of you. Do not think about them - simply feel, experience and enjoy.

"I AM LIGHT" – RITE 1

Commence your ritual standing, ensuring that you are perfectly aligned from head to toe. Place your hands in prayer position to your heart. Focus your attention on the energy of this affirming statement 'I am light'. Embrace and invite the pure light of healing and consciousness into the whole of your being.

Allow a feeling of expansiveness and visualise, feel or pretend to (feel and visualise) this brilliant light permeating the whole of your body - a shining light that flows into your head, your face and down your neck into your shoulders, arms and hands.

This light fills the whole of your back and the front of your torso, infiltrating the internal organs with healing light and down into the hips and buttocks and then into your legs and feet.

Feel this light energy moving into the earth connecting and grounding you to your life and all aspects of your being. Take a few moments before you begin to spin to become this light, breathing in the light.

This intention will set up the energy of light and healing that will stay with you throughout your entire practice. Affirm 'I am light' and you are ready to begin. Detailed instructions on this Rite are described in the following chapter.

"I AM HERE" – RITE 2

Lying down on the floor with your body aligned - affirm 'I am here'. Feel every muscle, bone, tissue, organ; your skin and the whole of your body, mind and emotions 'are here' in this present moment.

As you become fully 'here' your mind becomes still and this allows an awareness of a connection to every cell of your body. Nothing exists other than you, lying on the floor experiencing your self in the here and now. This wakes up your entire being and awareness to the truth that in reality there is nothing other than the here and now.

Allow yourself to feel an aliveness and a relief that no matter what is going on in your life and in your mind, it does not affect or influence you here and now, for in this moment you are here. 'I am here' and it is perfect. In time you will be able to feel 'here' in every moment and when the mind drifts to stress and worry, which can only exist in the past or the future, you will naturally and habitually move your attention to 'I am here'.

"I AM LOVE" – RITE 3

Position yourself ready for Rite 3 on your knees, once again ensuring that your body is aligned. Affirm 'I am love' and feel this primarily in your heart. Feel and experience your heart expanding. Lead with your heart and open your chest feeling the love flowing in. Be the love.

You are love and everything in the universe is love. In time you will think, feel, speak and listen from your heart. The energy of love is powerfully healing and in time an awareness will grow within you to feel the love and the truth of the light of love.

Love does not judge, love does not feel stress; love is who you are. State 'I am love' and attune yourself to this energy and really feel the reality of your being and your heart opening and softening with a deep peace and joy. With this openness you will be more flexible and it will allow your mind to reprogram all the negative chatter to one of harmony and love.

"I AM STRENGTH" – RITE 4

Sitting upright with the legs extended and spine aligned, take a moment to really feel and affirm, 'I am strength'. To activate this energy powerfully whilst you are sitting, engage your arms, (that are by your sides) and press your hands firmly into the floor feeling the muscles of the arms contracting and strengthening. Do this with your legs by flexing the feet and drawing your toes towards your body. Digging your heels into the floor - the backs of the knees will slightly lift off the floor. Draw your shoulders down, lift your chest then lead with the chest to flatten your back. Tighten and contract the whole of your body as you affirm 'I am strength'.

Feel and experience this strong energy in every part of your body. Your mind is focused on being strong and resilient, your emotions stable and balanced and your energy invokes this universal strong life force by breathing in strength and an abundance of prana will ensure that you perform this Rite with an effortless strength. You are now ready for the execution of this Rite and to experience empowerment.

"I AM FLOW" – RITE 5

On your hands and knees begin to engage the energy of 'I am flow' by affirming it. Take a few moments to breathe rhythmically as with all the Rites in and out of the nose. Really feel the flow of the breath and visualise expanding the whole of your body with the in breath and relax and let the breath flow out on the letting go feeling of the out breath.

Allow this free flow of energy to move through you like the waves of the ocean, flowing in and receiving the universal life force and flowing out, giving of the universal flowing life force to your life and all that exists. Feel your mind flowing freely and your emotions flowing, accepting and releasing.

Everything energetically in the universe flows in and out. Your body and the whole of your being flows in and out in harmony and in tune. This 'I am flow' statement will invoke a clearing on all levels and help you to get in touch with a pranic flow that is profoundly healing to all the inner pathways. Stay with this feeling and as you practise this Rite and in time you will flow freely and effortlessly.

"I AM CREATION" – RITE 6

Standing up and once again ensuring you are aligned - affirm 'I am creation'. Feel and visualise a creative energy permeating the whole of your body and being.

As you move into this Rite feel and move precisely and creatively. As you bend forward to activate this creative energy on the in breath suck your abdominals in and connect to the core of your creativity. Then as you hold your breath in, move creatively from side to side.

Experience and really feel this energy as you breathe out coming up to standing, allowing a creative flow to move up through your body and out of the crown of the head. Feel and be 'creation' for this in truth is what you are - a beautiful individual expression of the creative universal life force. This energy will release a creativity, which is already within you to fulfill the tapestry of life.

"I AM DIVINE" – RITE 7

As you position yourself for the headstand, placing the crown of the head to the floor ensuring that you are executing this Rite precisely, affirm 'I am divine' and feel the crown chakra opening and activating.

Visualise and experience a light just beyond the centre of the head and as you execute this pose allow this divine light to flow down into the whole of your body reaffirming 'I am divine'. This energy activates an energy of oneness, where no concept or notion of separation exists. You are one with all that is.

When you gently release from this pose and after a rest, sit with a straight back and allow yourself to feel and experience the energy of your divinity, perfect and one with all.

You are ready now to lie down and affirm 'I am surrender'. This pose is not classically a Rite yet a very important part of your ritual. Allow 5 to 10 minutes to surrender your body, emotions, mind and completely relax your muscles. Continue to affirm this statement and feel and experience a complete letting go, surrendering and surrendering. This allows a deep relaxation, which heals and regenerates you on all levels.

This pose and affirming 'I am surrender' is to be done after your practice regardless of what stage of the program you are in. You are now ready for Rite 8. Continue to affirm this statement and feel and experience a complete letting go, surrendering and surrendering. This allows a deep relaxation, which heals and regenerates you on all levels.

This pose and affirming 'I am surrender' is to be done after your practice regardless of what stage of the program you are in. You are now ready for Rite 8.

"I AM JOY" – RITE 8

As per instruction in the following chapter sit comfortably in a meditation position. Affirm with ease and from your heart 'I am joy'. Feel your heart expanding and experience a joy filling the whole of your being. Every cell of your body is joyous.

Feel and visualise billions of bubbles of pure joy permeating every aspect of your mind, emotions, your energy and physical body bathing in the energy of joy. Keep affirming this joy so that you feel or visualise an expansive bliss consciousness bathing and healing you from head to toe inside and out - your aura expanding infinitively to the light of joy.

Be joyous and know that this is your birthright and divine joy is who you really are. Joy will manifest into your life with practise and no matter where you are or what you are doing, choose joy. By choosing and affirming 'I am joy' in every moment of your life regardless of the circumstance will in time - with discipline, attract joyous circumstances. This affirmation, this choice has been known for centuries by the ancients to be the most profoundly healing energy known to humanity. So connect to this universal energy and be joy!

CHAPTER 3 the power of I am

Now with this awareness and focus you are ready to learn the Rites for Life exercises with a presence of light, love, strength, flow, creativity and divine joy.

learning the rites

1-5

chapter 4
learning the rites

OPEN YOUR HEART

The *Rites for Life* are exercises that open the inner channels, which include the seven major chakras and the thousands of energy channels called nadis. This creates a stronger, more flexible body, a calm and strengthened nervous system and a clearer mind. When all these systems work together in harmony, this allows for your heart to open.

So what does it mean to have an open heart? Many enlightened sages of the past recognised that your real self, the divine, is found in the deep recesses of the heart centre, also known as the Anahata Chakra. The heart centre is the direct path to the self, which has an awareness of the beauty and purity within everyone and everything. The experience of this connection and awareness is one of unconditional love and joy. The inner heart has no concept of separateness, it has a knowing that we are one and in the here and now.

The Rites are from a Tantric lineage. 'Tantra' is a system devised to enliven, expand and clear the chakras. This is done so that a powerful source of universal life force can flow to clear and release blockages for the preparation of the first stage of enlightenment. As the blockages clear, an expansiveness is experienced which creates the flow of a deep spiritual energy known as Shakti.

When in balance, energy flows through the body, and emotions flow in and out. When the energy is stuck, just like a blocked pipe, it cannot flow and release, resulting in stuck putrid matter in the pipe.

When energy is blocked the emotional, mental and physical bodies fill with pollutants and disease can occur. Practising these tantric exercises clears the nadis so energy flows in and out as nature intended. When this flow is experienced you have boundless energy, and a feeling of being enlivened or enlightened. When energy flows unobstructed a consciousness reveals itself. You find your true nature hidden under all the garbage. The light within you can shine and the light of awareness which was always there manifests.

Next, is a detailed explanation of these tantric techniques. They are to be done precisely as instructed and to be practised on a daily basis. Take your time to ensure you have understood the instructions and complete program before you commence.

rite 1

Rite for Light - Spinning

"I AM LIGHT"

"I AM LIGHT"

The first Rite activates the chakras and starts the cleansing process. The statement "I am light" connects you to the first Rite, which connects you to the energy of the spinning of the chakras. Everything in the universe is made up of spinning particles of light. Every atom in your body is made up of spinning light. Affirming the statement "I am light" while practising the first Rite helps you to be aware of the structure of your whole being.

Affirming "I am light" not only focuses the mind, it also activates the feeling and conviction that you are light energy. This helps to enliven every cell of the body. When tired, stressed or sick the cells of the body aren't functioning at their optimum, which inhibits the natural healing process. Saying "I am light" fills the cells of the body with a pranic, healing light and enhances the effect of the spinning and the rest of your practice.

rite 1

Rite for Light - Spinning

"I AM LIGHT"

SPINNING

The first Rite involves spinning in a clock-wise direction. It creates an opening and expansion of your chakras that continues to clear and cleanse the energy bodies.

Since this exercise sets up the clearing and opening of the chakras it has to be done precisely. When the body is stressed, sick and lacking in energy, the spinning of the chakras is slow which slows down the cleansing process. This causes premature ageing and a disconnection to the innate energies within and without. It is like a washing machine spinning at half speed and not cleaning the clothes effectively. The faster the spinning the more effective the dirt is spun off. It is the same with our chakras.

Before you spin, centre yourself, standing straight with the spine aligned. Tilt your pelvis slightly forward if there is an exaggerated curvature in the small of your lower back. Put your hand in prayer position resting at your heart and affirm "I am light" within or out loud three times.

The spinning needs to be practised as quickly as possible to start the healing process. Many people experience a dizzy disorientation and may lose balance when they first begin. If you are not used to spinning a sick feeling may arise in the stomach. This is an indication that the release is taking place. The *Rites for Life* program is designed to be practised one step at a time until the exercises are performed as they were intended. Modifications are required for some and don't be disheartened or discouraged if you need to start slowly.

You have begun the process and are addressing it wisely by moving at your own level. It does not take long before you clear the particular blockage and are able to spin quickly. The spinning also opens up the knee chakras, which is the energy connected to surrender. As all the chakras start to spin they unblock and encourage a surrender, a letting go of all that stands in the way of your purpose.

Stand with your legs hip-width apart and extend the arms at shoulder height, palms facing downward. Look to the left at a focal point and spin to the right, in a clockwise direction. Keep returning to that focal point with each spin to help you count. You can also focus on the tip of your middle finger on your left hand as you spin to the right to help with balance. Ensure that you are breathing smoothly and gently while spinning.

When you are first learning the *Rites for Life* only perform 7 repetitions of each Rite. Spin seven times, being careful that your knees are soft and that you pivot on one foot whilst the other foot propels you. Spin in a clockwise direction staying on the same spot, being careful not to lose your balance.

When you have finished spinning with the arms extended, bring your index fingers of both hands to your heart centre. Focus here for a moment with fingers together pressing firmly on the heart centre on the centre of the chest just under the breastbone. Release two strong 'HAHH' breaths, in through the nose and out of the mouth. If you are feeling off balance or sick after spinning keep focusing on the forefingers at the heart while doing releasing breaths, until the feeling stops.

MODIFICATION

A modified version of this Rite is to spin slowly to start with and after a while speed up the spins to your own level. If you find that you do not stay on the same spot whilst spinning then this is an indication for you to slow down.

If you still feel off balance after slowing down, then omit the spin for now and do the other Rites. After a while you will be able to include the spinning when you are more in balance. Keep in mind that the spinning should become as fast as possible to get the chakras open and regain a natural open spinning vortex of energy.

PRECAUTIONS:

- *Spin very slowly, or omit spinning if you have low or high blood pressure.*
- *Do not do this Rite if you are pregnant as spinning is a cleansing process.*
- *If you've had a knee replacement or knee injury (past or present) be very careful, and spin slowly with knees bent.*
- *If you've taken any recreational drugs or alcohol within 24 hours don't do the spinning as it is cleansing so it can cause an adverse reaction. After you have been practising the Rites for Life for a while an occasional small glass of wine with food and plenty of water should have no adverse affect, depending on the individual mind/body type.*

BENEFITS

Physical
- *Strengthens the muscles around the knees*
- *Activates the core muscles*

Emotional
- *Clears emotional resistances*
- *Expands the emotional body*
- *Heightens positive emotions*
- *Balances the emotions*

Mental
- *Sets up an energy to clear the mind*
- *Creates clarity and focus*
- *Balances the mind*
- *Clears the mental chatter*
- *Creates greater awareness of energy*

Spiritual
- *Connects you to light*
- *Clears all the other chakras for access to the spiritual*
- *Raises vibration*
- *Promotes surrender*
- *Opens the crown chakra*

rite 2

Rite for Here - Leg Raises

"I AM HERE"

"I AM HERE"

This Rite activates the throat chakra and the second chakra. The statement 'I am here' allows the mind to be fully present and brings you into a moving meditative state. Affirming 'I am here' engages every aspect of your body and stops the mind from wandering.

The statement also brings every cell of the body to attention in the here and now to be more receptive to the toning and strengthening of the body. This statement can be used at any time, and is particularly useful in times of stress for this is an indication that the mind is busy. Affirming this statement while performing the second rite stills the mind and increases the effectiveness of all the Rites because of your focused attention on being present.

rite 2

Rite for Here - Leg Raises
"I AM HERE"

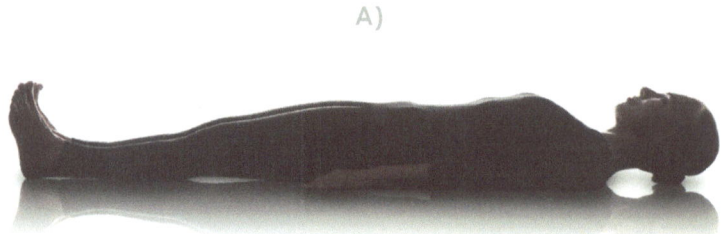

A)

STAGE 1 | LEG RAISES

Energetically this Rite activates the throat chakra, which relates to the thyroid and parathyroid glands that govern the metabolism. It also lengthens the back of the neck which releases tension here

This exercise also activates the second chakra, the sacrum area, which relates to your sex hormones and reproductive system. The lower abdominal core muscles are strengthened and toned. The second Rite also lengthens and stretches the hamstrings, which in turn releases tightness in the lower back. Rite 2 generally strengthens, tones and conditions the legs and torso.

A) Lying down on your mat face up, palms facing down, align your body, checking that both sides are even and your lower back is connected to the floor. Turn your body on by flexing the feet and contracting the muscles of the legs. Now engage the arms and hands by pressing them into the floor.

Affirm out loud or within 'I am here' and really feel that you are here, fully present.

B)

B) While inhaling for the count of four, lift both legs off the ground ensuring that the whole spine is on the floor and engaging the abdominal muscles. To ensure your back muscles are not doing the lifting, focus on lifting from the abdominals, holding for two breaths affirming 'I am here' as you suck your belly in. Breathing out for four releasing the legs down carefully as you press the spine into the floor.

Hold the breath out as you rest your legs and spine into the floor for two breaths and then inhaling deeply for the 4 breaths to continue your 7 repetitions if you are a beginner. As you raise your legs, you raise your head off the floor and tuck the chin into the upper chest. Keep your arms and hands pressed firmly into the floor.

It is vitally important that you are mindful of your back and neck to ensure no strain or injury. If you are straining, this is indication that you need to modify this exercise temporarily. As you progress, be ensured that you will get stronger. It is counter-productive to force or try too hard as it can cause injury and block the healing energy flow. Trying blocks prana.

If you notice any clicking in the hip or shoulder joints, don't be alarmed as this is an indication that your synovial fluid is low. The nature of the exercise will stimulate the fluid.

MODIFICATIONS

It is imperative that you are aware if your back arches of the floor. If so then experiment with these few modifications and determine which one suits you. Effortless effort is required. Another indication that you are trying too hard is if the breath is laboured.

Modification 1:
Raising one leg at a time does alleviate back and neck strain. Do the exercise exactly the same way except lift one leg, release it, and then raise the alternate leg.

Modification 2:
If the back still arches off the floor with one leg raising at a time then tuck the hands under the small of the back ensuring that you are not using the back muscles.

Modification 3:
If the former two modifications still feel strained, then bend the knees and bring them close to the chest as you inhale. As you exhale bring your feet to the floor. Keep your spine connected to the floor throughout.

If your neck feels stiff then simply keep your head on the floor throughout the exercise. The neck muscles will strengthen over time and you can then start slowly to lift the head.

When you have finished your repetitions take two deep releasing breaths, in through the nose and out of the mouth. Allow yourself to express a sound that represents how you feel. A long, strong "Hahhh" or an aggressive sounding one if that feels right. Sometimes you will feel at peace then release a soft "hah". The more you tune into how you are feeling and express that which you feel the more you will release.

After the Rite, hug your knees to your chest then roll over on your right side and come to kneeling for Rite 3.

BENEFITS

Physical

- *Strengthens inner core muscles*
- *Tones upper and lower abdominal regions*
- *Lengthens the hamstrings*
- *Strengthens the legs*
- *Stretches the lower back*
- *Lengthens the back of the neck*
- *Regulates metabolism*
- *Massages the internal organs*
- *Advanced version lengthens the spine*
- *Expands your breath capacity*

Emotional

- *Shifts you out of lethargy*
- *Connects you to the body*
- *Stabilises the emotions*
- *Grounding*
- *Encourages expression*

Mental

- *Focuses the mind*
- *Clears the mind*

Spiritual

- *Opens the second chakra (the sacral)*
- *Opens the fifth chakra (throat region)*

rite 2

Rite for Here - Leg Raises
"I AM HERE"

A)

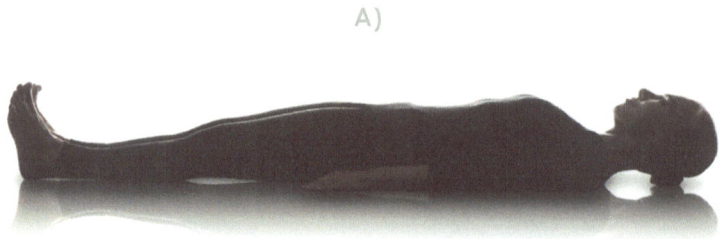

STAGE 2 | LEG RAISES WITH PLOUGH

This is the advanced version that you will build up to in time. Please do not attempt this until you have completed the full program or you practise yoga on a regular basis because you can create misalignment of the spine.

Lying on your back as instructed with Stage 1. Breathe in for a count of 4. Raise your legs keeping the spine on the floor, feeling vertebrae by vertebrae as you gently raise your legs to a point where you can lift your hips off the floor engaging your abdominal muscles. Continue to release the legs back over your head as far as your spine will allow you to.

Remember no forcing or straining. It may take time to be able to get the legs to the floor over your head. Keep your feet flexed and your legs strong and straight.

CHAPTER 4 learning the rites

Hold for two, repeat the statement 'I am here' and then slowly as you breathe out gradually for the count of 4, return the legs back the floor, vertebrae by vertebrae, ensuring the spine does not arch off the floor.

PRECAUTIONS:

- *For herniated disc, knees must be bent, and if there is still discomfort omit altogether.*
- *Any spinal operations or spinal concerns, consult your physician before commencing the practice.*
- *If there are any neck injuries keep the head down in line with the spine.*
- *Generally if there is any discomfort in the spine do a modified version.*
- *For extremely overactive thyroid until the condition stabilises keep the head down and do not raise it to meet the chest.*

rite 3

Rite for Here - Back Arch

"I AM LOVE"

"I AM LOVE"

Rite 3 focuses on opening up the heart chakra. To enhance awareness, the "I am love" statement permeates the truth that you are love. Affirming 'I am love' connects us to a higher vibration of universal love and a deeper connection within.

This statement gives the ability for a non-judgmental, full acceptance of self, which naturally flows to everyone else in your life. The more love vibration within you the healthier you become.

rite 3

Rite for Love - Leg Back Arch

"I AM LOVE"

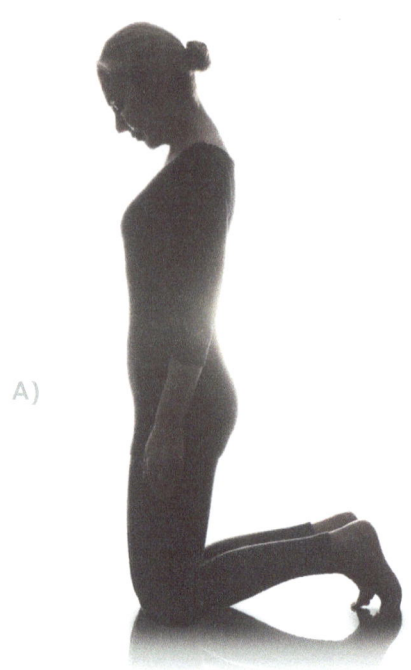

A)

BACK ARCH

This Rite also creates flexibility of the spine, releasing tightness in the shoulders as well as opening the chest and solar plexus area.

A) Kneel with feet hip width apart, with the toes tucked under. Arms are behind you with your hands tucked under the buttocks which helps to align your back.

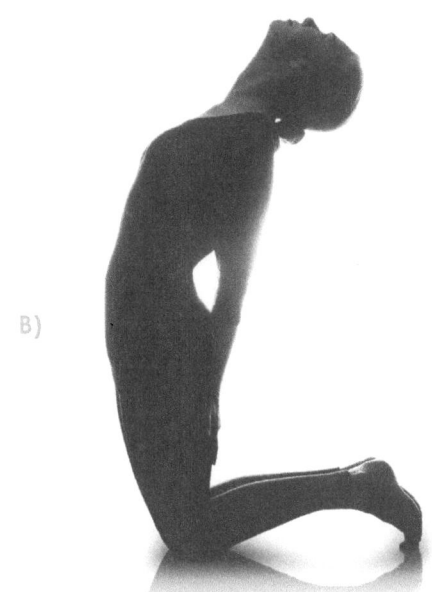

B)

B) Tuck your chin to chest and breathing in roll back the shoulders, tilt the pelvis so that it is in line with the knees and arch the spine. Carefully release the head back in line with the spine. Breathe in for 4 counts as you arch back. Hold the pose for a count of two squeezing the buttocks, affirming the statement 'I am love'.

Breathing out to return to the starting position with emphasis on the chin tucked into the chest, holding the breath out and suck the belly in. Finish with two deep releasing breaths.

MODIFICATION

If your neck feels stiff or uncomfortable, keep the chin tucked into the chest. Do not arch back too far, only as far as you feel comfortable. Tuck a thin blanket or pillow under the knees if you are feeling pressure in your knees.

PRECAUTIONS:

- *For any knee concerns, or if this Rite feels painful, omit it until the knee condition improves.*
- *For discomfort of the knees, place a folded up blanket (or roll up your mat) for extra padding under the knees.*
- *If there is any pain or discomfort anywhere along the spine, arch back very slightly and if discomfort persists, work with the breath and keep the back straight with the head and neck in line with the spine.*

BENEFITS

Physical

- *Creates greater flexibility for the spine*
- *Stretches the front of the torso*
- *Tones buttocks*
- *Lifts the chest*
- *Tones the bust*
- *Releases tension in the shoulders*
- *Stretches the front of the neck*
- *Expands your breath capacity and lungs*
- *Stimulates glands to increase metabolic rate*

Emotional

- *Creates a sense of joy*
- *Helps feelings of openness*
- *Calming effect*

Mental

- *Enhances focus*
- *Greater ability to be present*
- *Calms the mind*
- *Expands the mind*

Spiritual

- *Opens the heart chakra*
- *Opens the joy centre*
- *Opens the second and third chakras (sacral and solar plexuses)*
- *Allows surrender*

rite 4

Rite for Strength - Table Top

"I AM STRENGTH"

"I AM STRENGTH"

Rite number 4 opens your solar plexus. You may experience extra heat in the body with this exercise, which is the healing pranic energy building. It is like a fire within that burns off all dross and unwanted energies. This Rite requires you to exert your strength. The 'I am strength' statement really helps connect you to a universal strength that is your birthright.

You will find that this gives you powerful energy to perform this rite effortlessly. To tap into the strength within allows us to have a resilience and courage to deal with any circumstance that requires strength. Stress depletes our strength, affirming 'I am strength' does reduce the anxieties and insecurities within the mind and emotions. 'I am strength' sends the message to every cell and muscle of the body for effective toning. It is connecting the message of strength to all aspects of your being.

rite 4

Rite for Strength - Table Top

"I AM STRENGTH"

TABLE TOP

Rite 4 also strengthens the large muscle groups including the buttocks, back, legs, arms, shoulders and core. This powerful pose also tones your upper arms, legs, buttocks and the muscles of the back.

A) Sitting on the floor with legs straight and hip width apart, make sure that the body is aligned so the left side and the right side of the body are even. Arms are by the hips, palms facing downward with fingers together.

CHAPTER 4 learning the rites

B)

B) As you breathe in for 4 counts affirm 'I am strength', dig the heels into the floor and lift the hips in line with your shoulders, and gently release the head back. Holding for 2 counts squeeze the buttock, keeping all four points of the feet and toes pressed into the floor.

Make sure your knees don't splay when you come up to the tabletop position, that they keep in line with your ankles, and that your feet face forward. It's important that you keep the tabletop position by not arching your back if you have the flexibility or allowing the back to sag because you may not have the strength as yet.

Exhale for 4 counts, release back into the original position, holding the breath out for 2 counts as you draw your naval back towards your spine to activate your core muscles. When you have finished your repetitions take two deep releasing breaths.

MODIFICATION

At first this Rite may be a challenge. You may place your hands further back behind the hips or adjust your position to suit your comfort. Separating the feet a little wider may also help you with raising the hips off the floor. You may want to reduce the repetitions with this Rite until you get stronger, for example if you have just started the program and are doing 7 repetitions you may want to do only 3 of this fourth Rite. Know that you will get stronger.

PRECAUTIONS:

- *If you have any neck concerns, do not release the head back.*
- *If you have any knee concerns, make sure that you keep your knees in line with your ankles.*
- *If you have discomfort in your wrists, take note of the modification. If there is injury in the wrist or hands, omit this exercise until your condition improves.*

BENEFITS

Physical
- Tones and strengthens the arms
- Firms and lifts the buttocks
- Strengthen the wrists
- Promotes strength in the legs and back
- Increases stamina
- Increases energy
- Deepens the breath
- Activates core muscles
- Stretches the ankles
- Activates the feet and toes
- Weight bearing – strengthens your bones

Emotional
- Creates emotional strength
- Creates equilibrium
- Builds resilience

Mental
- Clarity
- Strong mind
- Greater mental capacity
- Endurance

Spiritual
- Opens the solar plexuses
- Activates the second chakra (sacral)
- Clears the energy channels
- Promotes healing energy
- Enhances pranic energy
- Creates spiritual energy (Shakti)

rite 5

Rite for Flow - Downward/Upward Facing Dog

"I AM FLOW"

"I AM FLOW"

Rite 5 is known as the downward facing dog / upward facing dog. The movement creates a greater strength and flexibility for the spine and the whole of your back. The upward movement opens the chest and gets you in touch with an effortless flow of energy. Everything in the universe flows in and out, like the waves of the ocean and your breath, in and out. The moon and the sun have their rhythm and flow in and out depending on the time of the day. When you use the statement 'I am flow' as you practise this Rite it deepens your connection to the flow of energy.

We are here to experience every single possible emotion for our learning. The statement 'I am flow' allows you to experience emotions and let them go. When the flow is out of balance, our emotions remain stuck. Affirming the 'I am flow' statement encourages a full experience of an emotion for learning and equally the releasing of it.

Emotions are meant to flow in and out for balance and harmony. When we get in touch with the energy of flow we naturally start to drink more water for this helps to release stuck emotions. Water is a conductor of energy which helps to release, on all levels, that which is to flow out. This statement encourages the energy that runs within the spine to flow freely and clear the chakras.

rite 5

Rite for Flow - Downward/Upward Facing Dog

"I AM FLOW"

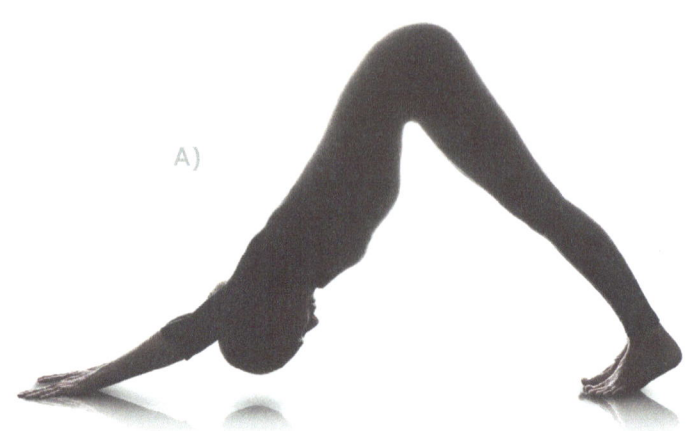

A)

DOWNWARD/UPWARD FACING DOG

Start the practice on your hands and knees with your arms shoulder-width apart, and at a 45-degree angle to your wrists. It's important that you experiment with the distance of your hands from your body to ensure that when you flow up into the dog pose your tail bone is pointing upward with the pelvis tilted creating a nice inverted 'V' shape. Ensure fingers are together with special attention to pressing the pads of the fingertips into the floor, particularly your thumbs. This engages the meridian that activates the shoulders.

A) Knees and feet hip width apart with toes tucked under. Keep the feet facing forward, not pointing in or out. This effects the foundation of your body. Inhaling for a count of 4 affirm the statement 'I am flow, and lift hips with tail bone pointing up towards ceiling and work with dipping the spine like a dog stretches, working towards pressing the heels down into the ground, feeling a lengthening in the achilles, the calves and the hamstrings. Keep the arms and legs straight and suck the belly in as you hold the pose for a count of 2.

CHAPTER 4 learning the rites

B) Keep the belly engaged as you move to upward facing dog. Exhaling for a count of four, flow into upward facing dog, keeping your toes tucked under, arms and legs are straight with an arch in the spine keeping the buttocks engaged. Release the head back, opening up the chest and throat, holding the breath out for two.

Continue to flow into the downward facing dog on the next inhalation ensuring you tuck your chin firmly into the chest and continue. It's important to tuck your chin right into your neck to lengthen the back of the neck for a counter-pose for arching the neck back.

C)

MODIFICATION

C) If you feel any discomfort by arching the back then do the plank pose on exhalation, instead of upward facing dog. Plank pose involves keeping the back straight, rather than arching back. After each Rite remember to do the releasing breaths. In through the nose and out of the mouth, making an audible sound, "HAH!!!".

PRECAUTIONS:

- *If there is any back injury, do not arch the spine.*
- *If you suffer from low blood pressure, do this pose very slowly, keeping your eyes opened and on a focal point.*

BENEFITS

Physical

- *Stretches the hamstrings*
- *Opens up the lower back*
- *Tones the arms*
- *Strengthens the shoulders*
- *Creates greater flexibility for the spine*
- *Establishes a rhythmical flow*
- *Opens the chest area*
- *Lengthens the front of the torso*
- *Stretches the lower and upper abdominal region*
- *Weight bearing – strengthens your bones*
- *Tones the neck*
- *Elongates the whole body*

Emotional

- *Harmony*
- *Unblocks the emotional body*
- *Feeling of being in flow*
- *Feel more connected*

Mental

- *Start to become more aware of energy*
- *Effortless focus*

Spiritual

- *Frees up the energy channels*
- *Opens the base chakra*
- *Creates energetic flow right along the spine and clears all the chakras*

REST AND ASSIMILATE

It is very important to lie down after you have completed your first five Rites regardless of how many repetitions you are doing. Do this for at least ten minutes. Resting after you have worked your body, activated your chakras and opened your energy channels allows for all that is still processing to release, settle and assimilate.

Make sure you body is aligned, palms facing upwards; feet gently flopped out by the sides. Completely let go of any muscular tension, be mindful of the breath and allow it to slow down.

To keep the mind present and assist the resting process and the ability to let go affirm 'I am surrender'. Then feel yourself softening, letting go and surrendering. The more you surrender the greater the healing will be. This also prepares you to go about your daily life having allowed the energies to settle and for you to be grounded.

CHAPTER 4 learning the rites

learning the rites

6-8

rite 6

Rite for Creation - Standing Twist

"I AM CREATION"

Once you can comfortably practise 21 repetitions of the first 5 Rites you are ready to learn Rite 6. Start with 7 repetitions only and remember to lie down after you have completed your practice to relax and surrender.

"I AM CREATION"

This Rite activates the second chakra, the creative centre. By affirming the powerful statement "I am creation", you are working with the awareness that you are the creator of your reality. Everything in your life, in the Universe, all that exists, is a creation. Affirming this statement allows you to tap into the creative force that you have within. This will help you to connect with your special gifts and express them.

The creator energy promotes an awareness that you truly are a creator of your reality. Because of the nature of these Rites, your creations will be in harmony with your highest good. Any blockage in the second chakra particularly on the physical level with the creation energy will start to heal and harmonise. For example women with hormonal issues, whether it is premenstrual or premenopausal, find greater ease and comfort. Men, often find that they become more in touch with this feeling creative centre. Be particularly aware of any resistance because of our conceptual conditionings. Remember whatever causes you to feel resistance is often your greatest gift once you surrender.

rite 6

Rite for Creation - Standing Twist

"I AM CREATION"

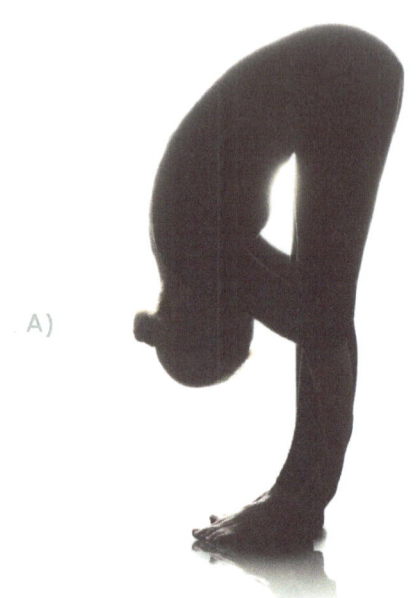

A)

STANDING TWIST

In this Rite the head is lower than the heart, which is extremely rejuvenating for the face and neck, providing a greater blood supply and stimulating the brain for greater oxygenation. It also works at stretching the hamstrings, opens and stretches the lower back, and massages the internal organs by the movement of the twist.

A) Stand with feet hip width apart, inhale and hinge from the hips, bring your body into a standing forward bend.

CHAPTER 4 learning the rites

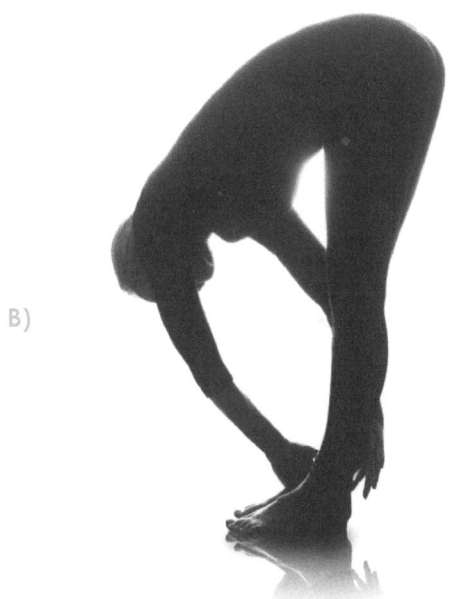

B)

B) Holding the breath rotate and place your hands behind the opposite ankle then return to the centre to repeat on the other side.

Now exhale and sucking your belly in come up to standing straight, hold the breath out for two and then repeat by breathing in and bending forward.

This Rite should only be practised 7 times initially. Build up slowly to the 21 repetitions. It is important not to feel any strain or discomfort in your lower back. Bend from the hips, work at releasing your chest as close as you can to your thighs without placing undue stress on your back.

MODIFICATION

If your hamstrings or lower back are feeling tight then to modify bend your knees. Remember the releasing breaths at the end of the repetitions and be aware that this Rite does require a greater capacity to breathe, know that this will be effortless with practise.

PRECAUTIONS:

- Any spinal concerns or discomfort, bend the knees and do not twist around as far.
- If you have high or low blood pressure do not do this Rite when the condition is extreme. A relatively low or high blood pressure requires a greater awareness in the movement.
- Make sure you breathe out fully as you come up to standing, and take your time to hold the out breath with the awareness at the crown of the head.
- Extra attention to sucking the belly in as you bend forward will ensure you don't over stretch your lower back.

BENEFITS

Physical
- *Profoundly stretches the hamstrings*
- *Tones the legs*
- *Releases tightness in the lower back*
- *Massages the lower intestinal tract*
- *Targets fatty deposits around the waist*
- *Encourages physical stability*
- *Greatly increases the breath capacity and breath retention*
- *Fuller oxygenation for the brain*
- *Increased blood flow to the face*

Emotional
- *Flexibility of the emotions*
- *Feeling of being centred*
- *Expansiveness*

Mental
- *Balances the right and left hemispheres of the brain*
- *Stimulates creativity*
- *Encourages lateral thinking*

Spiritual
- *Draws the energy up the spine and clears all the six chakras and opens the crown chakra*
- *Encourages kundalini energy*

rite 7

Rite for Divinity - Headstand

"I AM DIVINE"

Once you can comfortably practise 21 repetitions of the first 6 Rites you are ready to learn Rite 7. Start with 7 repetitions only and remember to lie down after you have completed your practice to relax and surrender.

"I AM DIVINE"

The headstand activates the crown chakra, allowing us to experience the reality that we are one with all. The statement 'I am divine' affirms the connection to everything. Once you start doing this rite and affirming this statement you move beyond your energetic, human component and connect to the spiritual dimension, which is beyond the mind, emotions and body.

If the crown is blocked it inhibits energy from being released, for the nature of energy flows up along the spine and out the crown of the head. Affirming the powerful message 'I am divine' reconnects us to the truth of who we really are.

rite 7

Rite for Divinity - Headstand

"I AM DIVINE"

A)

HEADSTAND

It is important that you do not do this Rite if you have a history of any neck concerns or have very weak abdominal muscles. If you are doing 21 repetitions of the first five Rites you may be ready to start with 7 repetitions of Rite 7 if your abdominals are strong enough. You will be doing this Rite initially close to a wall for when you need support to help you with your balance.

A) To begin, kneel close to a wall. Link your hands and place them at the middle of your head for support. Start to bend forward, placing your head on the ground. Adjust your head in-between the hands and straighten your legs, raising your hips and buttocks up. Start to walk your feet towards your hips.

CHAPTER 4 learning the rites

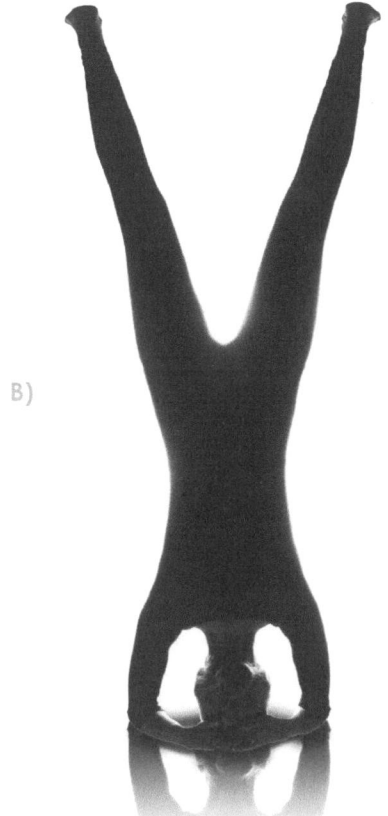

B)

B) Once you feel stable raise your legs until you are standing on your head. If you loose your balance bend the knees and place them on the wall. Take your time to get used to standing on your head and when feeling in balance release your feet from the wall. Inhale and move your legs apart with the feet flexed. As you hold your breath in you twist gently with the core muscles strongly engaged to one side and then the other. Exhale and bring your legs together with toes pointed and suck your belly in.

Rest after you have come out of this posture in pose of the child, which is the buttocks on heels and nose to the floor with arms by your sides. Then sit up and perform your releasing breaths twice.

MODIFICATION

Kneel and raise your buttocks with hands in-line with the shoulders, keeping your head and neck in line with the spine and count the required repetitions with the breaths.

After a while when you get used to having some pressure on your head you may be ready to have the legs resting on the wall still counting your breaths as the repetitions.

PRECAUTIONS:

- *Do not perform this Rite if you have weak abdominal muscles. If you are performing the complete program correctly you may have strengthened your abdominals. If not, continue the other Rites with a stronger focus and intent to strengthen the abdominal muscles. The more engaged your abdominal muscles are, the stronger your back.*
- *Do not perform this Rite if you have weak or impaired neck muscles. This can damage the cervical area.*
- *Do not perform this Rite if you have extremely low blood pressure or eye issues, such as glaucoma.*
- *If you have an extreme case of scoliosis this Rite may exacerbate the condition.*
- *Any spinal misalignment needs to be addressed before doing a headstand.*
- *Rest for a few minutes after the pose to allow the reversal of blood flow for reorientation.*

BENEFITS

Physical

- *Greater balance*
- *Engages core muscles strongly*
- *Strengthens neck*
- *Strengthens arms*
- *Strengthens the muscles of the back*
- *Increases the flexibility of the spine*
- *Stretches the inner thighs*
- *Massages the internal organs*
- *Slows your heart rate down*
- *Engages all the muscles of the body*
- *Fully oxygenates the brain*
- *Rejuvenating for the face and neck*
- *Stimulates the top of the head*

Emotional

- *Balances the emotions*
- *Calms the emotions*
- *Stability*

Mental

- *Strongly focuses the mind*
- *Shifts your perspective*
- *Clears the mind*
- *Creates greater equilibrium*
- *Creates greater ability to be more present*

Spiritual

- *Ability to experience oneness*
- *Opens the crown chakra*
- *Greater capacity to transcend*
- *Expansive*

rite 8

Rite for Joy - Smiling Meditation

"I AM JOY"

Once you can comfortably practise 21 repetitions of the first 7 Rites you are ready to learn Rite 8. Remember to lie down after you have completed Rite 7 to relax and surrender. Then you can sit up and complete Rite 8.

"I AM JOY"

This Rite is a healing meditation that requires you to sit and smile for up to 20 minutes while repeating the affirmation "I am joy". The meditation stimulates the thymus gland that is largely responsible for the immune system. The more joy you experience the healthier you become. Joy is the key to opening your heart. We are here to live a full life so choose joy regardless of your situation or circumstance and step into that beautiful powerful being that you are.

Affirming the statement "I am joy" allows you to experience a greater sense of joy and expansion. By approaching life with an energy of joy attracts a higher vibrational experience in life. Life flows with joy.

With the smiling meditation, when you smile with your eyes, the energy opens up the third eye and the crown centre. When you smile with your cheeks, it's connected to your throat, heart and solar plexus. It is important that after the expansiveness of the smiling meditation to give yourself a few moments to feel your body and to feel connected to the earth so that you feel grounded and can go about your day in a joyful way.

… # rite 8

Rite for Joy - Smiling Meditation

"I AM JOY"

SMILING MEDITATION

If sitting crossed legged is a challenge then you may sit on a chair, but do not rest your back against the back of the chair so you don't drift off to sleep and so your spine stays aligned. If you do have a weak back or spinal issues, feel free to rest your back against the back of chair or a wall yet make sure that your spine is as straight as possible. Sometimes it helps to place a pillow at the small of your back to ensure comfort and alignment.

To soften the face and relax the muscles, open your mouth as wide as possible two times. Make sure you are comfortable and able to sit for 20 minutes. If 20 minutes is a challenge, don't be discouraged, you can slowly build up from five minutes and still receive the benefits.

Beginners of meditation often experience feelings of physical discomfort. Please do not feel that you have to sit perfectly still for the whole time. If your body has an ache or needs to move, gently move the body, get comfortable and resume your meditation. This can be done several times throughout the meditation.

It's common for feelings of sadness and resistance to emerge. Don't give yourself a hard time about it, acknowledge the feelings, continue the practice and know that this is part of the stress releasing process. Often people feel more joyful after the practice.

When I started doing this meditation, it was at a difficult period in my life and I felt I had nothing to smile about as I had focused on finding a joy that was outside of me.

With practise, I discovered that there is a joy within that does not depend on anything. At first it was only a fleeting experience of joy, but it was a reference point and I know that I can return to that place regardless of what's going on. With time, the feeling of peace and joy builds and carries you through day-to-day life.

It is important with this meditation that you focus on the outer smile so you can bring it into your everyday life. The outer smile helps you to engage in what you are doing. Close your eyes, relax your cheeks and mouth. Smile with your eyes, your cheeks and your mouth, turning them all upwards.

If your face gets tired open your mouth nice and wide and stretch it out. Then go back to the mantra "I am joy". Give yourself permission to stretch your face as much as you need to. It's more disruptive to be uncomfortable. When the mind drifts from the awareness of the smile, simply go back to the experience of the smile. Each time the mind wanders, bring it back to the smile. Allow yourself to feel the joy that you have within.

What the smiling meditation does is consolidates the whole *Rites for Life* practice by bringing the light of joy into your chakras, into your experience, into every cell of your body.

100 reasons to practise

Rite for Joy - Smiling Meditation

PHYSICAL BENEFITS

1. It lowers oxygen consumption
2. It decreases respiratory rate
3. It increases blood flow and slows heart rate
4. Increases exercise tolerance
5. Leads to a deeper level of physical relaxation
6. Good for people with high blood pressure
7. Reduces anxiety attacks by lowering levels of blood lactate
8. Decreases muscle tension
9. Helps in chronic diseases such as allergies and arthritis
10. Reduces pre-menstrual syndrome symptoms
11. Helps in post-operative healing
12. Enhances the immune system
13. Reduces activity of viruses and emotional distress
14. Enhances energy, strength and vigour
15. Helps with weight loss
16. Reduction of free radicals, less tissue damage
17. Higher skin resistance
18. Drop in cholesterol levels, lowers risk of cardiovascular disease
19. Improved flow of air to the lungs resulting in easier breathing
20. Decreases the ageing process
21. Higher levels of DHEAS (Dehydroepiandrosterone)
22. Prevents, slows or controls pain of chronic diseases
23. Makes you sweat less
24. Cures headaches and migraines
25. Greater orderliness of brain functioning
26. Reduces need for medical care
27. Less energy wasted
28. More inclined to sports, activities
29. Significant relief from asthma
30. Improves performance in athletic events
31. Normalises to your ideal weight
32. Harmonises our endocrine system
33. Relaxes our nervous system
34. Produces lasting beneficial changes in brain electrical activity
35. Helps fertility (the stresses of infertility can interfere with the release of hormones that regulate ovulation)

MENTAL & EMOTIONAL BENEFITS

36 | Builds self-confidence
37 | Increases serotonin levels, influences mood and behaviour
38 | Resolve phobias and fears
39 | Helps control own thoughts
40 | Helps with focus and concentration
41 | Increases creativity
42 | Increases brain wave coherence
43 | Improves learning ability and memory
44 | Increases feelings of vitality and rejuvenation
45 | Increases emotional stability
46 | Improves relationships
47 | Mind ages at slower rate
48 | Easier to remove bad habits
49 | Develops intuition
50 | Increases productivity
51 | Improves relations at home and at work
52 | Able to see the bigger picture in a given situation
53 | Helps ignore petty issues
54 | Increases ability to solve complex problems
55 | Purifies your character
56 | Develops will power
57 | Greater communication between the two brain hemispheres
58 | React more quickly and more effectively to a stressful event
59 | Increases one's perceptual ability and motor performance
60 | Higher intelligence growth rate
61 | Increased job satisfaction
62 | Increase in the capacity for intimate contact with loved ones
63 | Decrease in potential mental illness
64 | Better, more sociable behaviour
65 | Less aggressiveness
66 | Helps in quitting smoking, alcohol addiction
67 | Reduces need and dependency on drugs, pills and pharmaceuticals
68 | Need less sleep to recover from sleep deprivation
69 | Require less time to fall asleep, helps cure insomnia
70 | Increases sense of responsibility
71 | Reduces road rage
72 | Decrease in restless thinking
73 | Decreased tendency to worry
74 | Increases listening skills and empathy

SPIRITUAL BENEFITS

80 | *Helps keep things in perspective*
81 | *Provides peace of mind, happiness*
82 | *Helps you discover your purpose*
83 | *Increases self-actualisation*
84 | *Increased compassion*
85 | *Growing wisdom*
86 | *Deeper understanding of yourself and others*
87 | *Brings body, mind, spirit in harmony*
88 | *Deeper level of spiritual relaxation*
89 | *Increased acceptance of oneself*
90 | *Helps to learn forgiveness*
91 | *Changes attitude towards life*
92 | *Creates a deeper relationship with self*
93 | *Attain enlightenment*
94 | *Greater inner-directedness*
95 | *Helps living in the present moment*
96 | *Creates a widening, deepening capacity for love*
97 | *Discovery of the power and consciousness beyond the ego*
98 | *Experience an inner sense of assurance or knowingness*
99 | *Experience a sense of oneness*
100 | *Increases the synchronicity in your life*

transform

chapter 5
releasing & clearing

Most people have emotional and mental blockages that start to release when they start doing the Rites. One of the reasons it's recommended that you start with doing just a few repetitions of the Rites, rather than the complete 21 repetitions, is so the releasing process is not too intense. Even so, after teaching thousands of people I've found that there are always some people who experience temporary discomfort because of the cleansing and healing process.

This involves the body throwing off the blockages that have been held for so long. Obviously this varies from individual to individual and the following information is a guideline to help you with your experience and progress of the Rites. I'm wary of giving you this information because I don't want to plant the seed of fear. Nevertheless it is important to be aware of what can happen with your energies so you know how to deal with them.

When you start doing the Rites your energies start spinning faster, like a washing machine throwing off unwanted matter. Mostly the unwanted matter that is being thrown off on a daily basis is unnoticeable and just keeps you feeling cleansed. Occasionally, once you start peeling away the layers you can come across a big stain and when it releases it can often be felt. It is important to realise that any discomfort that you experience when you are doing the Rites is not a coincidence. Some of the things that people have experienced, and that you may experience range from headaches to lower back pain.

HEADACHES - Third Eye Chakra

Headaches can often be experienced. This may be due to dehydration because the cleansing process requires water. When you are working with energy your body requires more water in order to facilitate the energy because water is a conductor of energy. If you do not drink the amount of water your body requires, then you can experience headaches.

Drink more water and the headaches should clear. The other possible reason for headaches is a blocked energy around the third eye chakra. When you do your releasing breaths between each Rite, breathe in through the nose and out the mouth. Whilst you do this visualise sending the discomfort in the head, which is a stuck energy, out the crown of the head. Do this a few times, continue your Rites and in most cases the discomfort will shift.

It is highly unlikely that the headache is something of a serious nature yet if it persists please consult your health practitioner.

Often energy can get stuck in the third eye chakra because you have not slowed your mind down and are still thinking and not being present in the body, so it is very important for you to feel your body, count your breaths and affirm your statements to prevent the mind chatter.

NECK TENSION - Throat Chakra

Some people experience extreme muscular tension in the neck. This may be due to two reasons. Firstly, you may not be used to using the neck muscles therefore it is as simple as exercising a part of the body that has been dormant for a while and the muscle tension is a result of the muscles getting stronger.

If you are experiencing neck tension my advice usually is to keep your head down, with your chin to chest, with most of the poses and rest your neck for a few days and then resume gently to work the neck muscles. You will find that you shift through this very quickly.

Secondly, particularly with Rite 3 (the back arch) when you are first learning this Rite it is a challenge to breathe in deeply as you release the head back. This can block the energy of the throat chakra and the muscles at the back of the neck are related to this centre.

TIGHT CHEST - Heart Chakra

Over the many years of running the Rites workshop, there have been a few cases of people feeling very tight in the chest. I remember a few cases where the person rang me after being in emergency all night to discover that they were not having a heart attack. After speaking with me they realised it was a very positive energy that was opening the heart.

I mention this to alleviate the fear when the heart chakra starts to open because it can hurt. If you are unsure of what is going on it is important to consult a physician yet in my experience I have always found it to be a release of some old grief. When the heart chakra starts to open as it does when you are doing the Rites some people also experience shoulder, chest or upper back pain. Also when the heart is opening, some people experience the feeling of a stabbing pain in the centre of the chest.

My advice is to deepen your breath whilst doing your Rites to shift the energy even if it feels uncomfortable. If too uncomfortable just do a few, slowly and mindfully with the breath and you will find this helps greatly. Allow yourself to see this as a wonderful thing; you are opening your heart.

NAUSEA - Solar Plexus Chakra

The solar plexus, your upper abdominal region, is the centre that stores fear and anxiety. I have often found that when this centre starts to open and release the fears and anxieties that it is normal to experience nausea. Providing you have not eaten a heavy meal just before doing the Rites, or had any alcohol, this nauseous feeling will dissipate as you continue with your practice. Take heart, you are opening up your solar plexus and releasing many of the daily and long-term anxieties.

You will find that when you move through this, and you do move through it, there is a sense of strength and empowerment that is taken into your day-to-day life. If the upper abdominal muscles have not been used much, then you may experience some upper abdominal muscle tightness and soreness, therefore breathe deeply, particularly whilst doing Rite 4 (the table top) which really opens the solar plexus and make sure you affirm 'I am strength'. In a very short time you will be strength.

LOWER BACK - Sacral Chakra

If there are any imbalances in the second chakra region, which is the area below the navel and the lower back, there can be discomfort here when blockages are releasing. This area relates to your hormones, large intestines and your creativity and sensuality. Often people who are blocked in this centre either physically or emotionally experience a feeling of a band of tightness or discomfort in this area.

If this is the case, it is very important not to over arch your back when your body is not ready. You may be over stretching causing the energy to be blocked. In most cases this discomfort in the lower abdominal and lower back region is caused by not doing Rite 2 (leg lift) correctly. Please be extra careful not to allow your lower back to lift of the floor and if so, you must do the modifications recommended. If you are doing your Rites correctly, and still experience lower abdominal and lower back pain, this is definitely an indication that you are releasing a blockage and if you continue with your practice after a few days, sometimes more or less, it will shift.

As with all the other Rites, ensuring deep rhythmical breathing is important. Your creativity, your sensuality, your feeling centre is opening up.

Most women find that they are comfortable doing the Rites whilst menstruating even on days when there is a heavy flow. I have found that the discomfort in menstruation dissipates as the second chakra opens. In menopause, women that do the Rites have a positive transition and are less likely to experience the common symptoms.

COCCYX - Base Chakra

When the base chakra starts to fully open because you are doing the *Rites for Life*, there are people who have experienced a pain at the tip of the coccyx where the base chakra resides because you are starting to awaken the kundalini energy, the energy then runs up along the spine to clear all blockages to clear a path for enlightenment.

This pain can be quite severe at times and is very unlikely to happen if you do your Rites everyday. I have found that stuck base chakra energy discomfort arises when somebody has stopped doing the Rites for a while and resumes them again.

What is happening with the energy when you are doing the Rites is you are opening the chakra and it is spinning nicely. When you stop all of a sudden, it can close the base chakra down. When people stop doing the Rites an indication that the base chakra is shut down is that they lose enthusiasm for life and even become quite depressed. Once they recognise this and start to do the Rites again the base chakra starts to open up and the pain is a result of that.

Once again breathing very deeply and if at any time you may experience extreme discomfort I suggest you breathe into the base as you are sitting on the floor, or even better on the earth, and then breathe out visualising the energy releasing up along the spine and out the crown. It is also very beneficial with your knees slightly bent, standing up, bounce up and down on your heels. This helps to reactivate the base chakra.

When there is discomfort in the base like this it is very rare yet it is a very positive indication that you have awakened the kundalini energy. For this reason alone, it is very important not to stop and start your Rites. It can be dangerous and play havoc with your energies. In saying that doing your Rites regularly, at your own pace, you are enlightening your whole being and any discomfort is only temporary if approached wisely.

chapter 6
abundant health

NUTRITION

When you start doing the Rites people find they naturally change their eating habits. People often find they gravitate towards higher vibrational foods, like fresh fruit and vegetables. They become aware of the life force in foods. There are no rules against meat eating, but meat can make your energy levels dense which means you are not as sensitive to energies. Heavy meat eaters are also in danger of not being aware of when energy is stuck.

I have found that digestion and elimination are the most important functions for good health. Your choice of food depends on your individual constitution and body type. For example a man that works physically with a strong muscular body type is more likely to digest heavy carbohydrates and proteins than a slight less active female. In most cases the male muscular body type will be able to digest and process heavier foods therefore not interfering as much with the energy of *Rites for Life*. If this slight female was to eat the same as the muscular male she would possibly find it very difficult to digest and eliminate effectively therefore blocking the free flow of energy throughout her body. Ideally regardless of body type high vibrational, live, energy-building foods enhance your healing process. The foods that are highest vibration are also the most nutritious; for example sprouts and fresh organic fruit and vegetables are highly nourishing and don't adversely affect the digestive system.

Heavy, unnatural foods require a lot of energy to be digested. You may notice that after overindulging that you have no energy. This is because most of your energy is going towards digesting and processing the heavy food. Eating too much, even if it is highly nutritious, can also drain the body of its energy reserves in order to process that food.

As you continue to practise the Rites for Life you will find that you will naturally gravitate to the foods that nourish you appropriately. This can change from day to day and week to week. Because you are practising the Rites for Life you become more aware and make the changes necessary for your body's individual requirements.

It's also important that you are mindful of how you eat. Chewing your food thoroughly until it becomes liquid is the most important step in digestion. It activates the acids used in digestion and extracts more vitamins and minerals from the foods that you eat as well as slowing your mind down and allowing you to enjoy the moment. When we chew our food thoroughly and drink with awareness we are able to extract more prana from the food to nourish ourselves on an energetic level.

In the process of regenerating with the *Rites for Life* you may find that food cravings arise. Often people say that people want to eat sugar, or quick release energy foods. It is very difficult to talk about the individual reactions and processes of the body yet if you find that you have sugar cravings, a simple tip is to eat a high quality protein like activated nuts. When you are healing you really need your protein. If you are not allergic, organic grain-fed eggs are a great source of protein, B vitamins and magnesium. Having a fermented substance like apple cider vinegar or pickles also helps those with weak digestion to help break down the protein.

A healthy body is alkaline. A sick, stressed, diseased body is highly acidic. You can do your own testing for your pH levels by buying a pH kit that measures your acid/alkaline balance. Eating foods that are alkaline like leafy green vegetables, promote healing for the body.

A highly acidic state is generally a toxic body. While it is very important to balance your alkaline / acid levels with good food, your stress levels can often undermine a highly alkaline diet. Many people that eat organically, vegetarian or vegan that don't drink alcohol or smoke can have highly acidic systems when experiencing extreme stress. To reduce the acid levels, you need to reduce the stress. This can be done with the *Rites for Life*.

I've studied and been interested in nutrition all my adult life. I've found that there have been a lot of discrepancies between the many diets and health foods and different crazes. I've done them all. My family are vegetarian so it was extremely important to me to provide a perfectly balanced diet. Over the years I've experimented with different fads from goji berries to coconut water, and find now that it is the assimilation of the food, and the elimination of waste that is key.

Assimilation is the ability to extract nutrition from the food that you are eating so that your body can absorb the nutrients. For effective assimilation you need to have the right balance of acids in your system. Apple cider vinegar in your diet can help with breaking down protein and carbohydrates so the body can absorb them. The way to ensure proper elimination is to eat whole, fibre-rich unprocessed foods including most fruits, vegetables, seeds, nuts and water.

I found that when I was being very strict and regimented that this restricted an expansion and openness of my mind. My emotions became rigid as well. Over the years I have learnt to relax about having a glass of wine occasionally, or a small piece of fish and have discovered that the enjoyment of the food, the company I'm with, my state of mind and what's happening in my life and how happy I am is more important than a regimented diet. I find that if I nourish myself emotionally and I'm happy with who I am, I can relax about the food that I eat, making sure that 80% of it is of nutritional value that I'm in good health. Even when I have times that I pick and don't eat, as I should, when my stress levels are low, it does not affect my health. I find stress to be the greatest killer and manifests itself in so many damaging ways.

HYDRATION

Water is a conductor of energy so if your body is dehydrated by not ingesting enough fluids you lose energy. Drinking purified, clean water is essential energetically to your system and aids in getting rid of toxins.

Most people to varying degrees are dehydrated. To encourage hydration of the cells it is a good idea to add a carrier to your water like fresh lemon juice or salt or a small amount of natural juice (but not orange juice).

SEXUAL ENERGY

There is a lot of misunderstanding associated with sexual energy and celibacy in relation to the *Rites for Life*; as they are a tantric practice that works with drawing the sexual base energy up for transmutation along the spine. There are some that say you have to be celibate in order to do the *Rites for Life*. If you are engaging in sex and climaxing frequently then you have less energy for the clearing process. In my opinion this is no reason not to do the *Rites for Life*.

If you are a serious tantric student then it is advisable not to dissipate your sexual energy but for everyone else, having sex is not going to interfere with your Rites.

The *Rites for Life* open up all the energy centres, which gives a feeling of being completely alive, 'turned on' in a way. From a yogic view it is important to be turned on, in every way, which also means being turned on sexually. Allow yourself to be turned on at all times for it is a life force that is within you. The Universe doesn't judge you, nor is it interested in how much or little sex you may have. What is important is that you keep the energy flowing through you to help with your rejuvenation. Those that have a strong life force usually appear to be younger than their years. The more turned on you are, the younger you will be!

RITES FOR LIFE & THE AGEING PROCESS

The *Rites for Life* disciplines the mind and body in preparation for higher states of awareness. The disciplines and techniques allow an actual experience of the interconnectedness of the whole being. One of the benefits of these disciplines is the mind and body are brought into harmony creating a perfect environment for health and well-being. A proven side effect of this enhanced well-being is a slowing or even reversal of the ageing process.

Reversal of the ageing process is not due to any one aspect of the *Rites for Life* program. The program is a complete science and perfect harmony and well-being will only be attained when all aspects are practised regularly.

These aspects include self-purification, asanas (postures), pranayama (breath control), relaxation techniques and meditation. Self-purification relates to motives, speech, action and care of the body.

Asanas

A primary component of the Rites are postures that increase flexibility, strengthen and tone the muscles, stimulate glandular activity, strengthen the nervous and immune system, massage the internal organs, lengthen the spine, rejuvenate the skin and purify the blood.

Pranayamas

Are breathing techniques practised in conjunction with the Rites that expand the lungs, oxygenate the blood, balance the metabolism, help with cellular regeneration, aid in digestion, create a healthy nervous system, control weight; align us with the energy of the Universe and help calm the mind.

Relaxation

Practised after the completion of the postures will reduce stress, release muscle tension, enhance the immune and nervous systems, relax the mind and allow a profound healing rest on a cellular level.

Meditation

The completion of the program is a spiritual practice that brings about peace, joy, love, detachment and the realisation that all is one.

When all these aspects are practised with the Rites for Life you will start to feel and look younger. When they are mastered you will realise you are and have always been perfect.

chapter 7
tips & consideration for your practice

ATTITUDE

Your attitude and thoughts whilst performing the *Rites for Life* are the key to your engagement with the cells of the body; the opening of your chakras; the tone, strength and flexibility of your body; and the healing of your whole being.

Being present and not allowing your mind to wander will help to relieve stress. With practise you will become more aware of the thoughts that clutter your mind. Your attitude affects the egos resistances and it will be explained further how to embrace the ego in the following chapter.

BREATHING

The Rites for Life are a tantric practice. The nature of them is to transmute energy in the body, mind and emotions that stands in the way of enlightenment. The execution of the practice is physical with a mind/body connection to the breath. Correct breathing is key to the success of the practice.

According to the Yogis there are three important aspects to correct breathing. Firstly, breathing in and out of the nose; this filters the air for a cleaner breath. Breathing in and out of the nose also allows us to extract more prana from the oxygen that we breathe because it activates the olfactory system (the system that allows you to smell). Mouth breathing dissipates the power of the pranic healing energy. Secondly, full diaphragmatic three-stage breathing is essential. This involves expanding on the in breath, allowing the lower abdominal region to rise as you breathe in. Then, as you continue to breathe in; the breath naturally expands the rib cage, and with that natural inhalation, the chest rises and expands.

Thirdly, breathing rhythmically is vitally important to extract the prana. This means the 'in' breath and the 'out' breath should be even and the breath retentions are half of the inhalations and exhalations. For example, breathing in for 4 counts, holding for 2 counts and breathing out for 4 counts, and holding the breath out for 2 counts. Holding the breath out for 2 counts is vitally important; for then you will find the next in breath is deeper and filled with more prana. Please do not be concerned about the details of the breath initially, simply have an awareness of the breath and you will find that by practising the *Rites for Life*, your breathing will naturally harmonise.

FOCUSED ATTENTION

To master any activity requires a focused mind. When the mind is fully present awareness expands and more universal energy flows to the point of attention. The techniques taught in the *Rites for Life* helps the mind to stay present. A focused attention on the exercise with synchronism of the breath is imperative yet not enough to keep the mind from wandering. Often there can be a background of chatter within the mind that can limit the mastery of the practice.

SEQUENCE

It is vitally important that you practise the *Rites for Life* in the correct order and not change the postures or the sequence in any way. They were designed specifically to allow the energy to flow in a balanced way and any deviation from this can create disturbances in your energy field. If you want to do other yoga poses, it is recommended that you do the *Rites for Life* before you do anything else.

FOOD, DRINK & DRUGS

As with most types of exercise, it is advisable not to eat at least an hour before the practice. If you require something to eat then choose something light that will not interfere with your healing process. The digestion of food takes up a lot of the body's energy leaving you less energy to do your practice. It is also not advisable to consume alcohol whilst learning the *Rites for Life*.

If you find that you are in a situation where you have consumed alcohol, please drink plenty of water and wait at least three hours after intake.

Prescription drugs that your doctor has recommended does not interfere with your practice, although this may vary with individuals who take anti-depressants. Please ask your health professional for advice before commencing the practice if you have any concerns. It is highly recommended not to take recreational drugs if you choose to work with the *Rites for Life* because it can lead to psychological imbalances and delusional experiences. Please don't underestimate the energetic power of the *Rites for Life*, and if misused, they can work against you.

WHEN TO PRACTISE

You may practise the Rites at any time of the day or evening, however it is advisable to do the *Rites for Life* first thing in the morning as this sets up a powerful, energetic day. If you are not a morning person, you can use the *Rites for Life* to cleanse your day and do them before your evening activities. You may also do them before you go to bed, yet some have experienced not being able to settle and sleep well. Some people report they do sleep exceptionally well so this is something for you to experiment with.

FREQUENCY

It is advisable to do the *Rites for Life* daily. The reason being is that we start to cleanse and release blockages and if we stop we can create a lot of discomfort as we may have been ready to release something and by stopping it remains stuck. Missing one day a week is acceptable but more than that is not recommended. Remember they are *Rites for Life*. Include them in your daily routine, like brushing your teeth.

PREGNANCY

If you have been practising the *Rites for Life* for a while and discover you are pregnant it is quite safe to do all the exercises except for the spinning. The spinning starts a cleanse which is not appropriate for pregnancy. In the later stages of pregnancy you may find that you need to do the modified version of each Rite. Having taught many pregnant women over the years, the *Rites for Life* have definitely kept their energy levels high, their body strong, emotions in balance, being able to deliver strong and healthy babies.

CHILDREN

It is not advisable for children to do the *Rites for Life* until their spine is fully grown nor without professional supervision.

REVISION

After you have been doing the *Rites for Life* for a while it's important to re-read the instructions occasionally to ensure that you are doing them correctly. It can be harmful, energetically and physically, to do the *Rites for Life* incorrectly. They are specifically designed to balance and align your energies and the body. I have found that often that when people first learn the *Rites for Life* and have adverse side effects, such as a sore back or neck or extreme emotional outbursts, they are not doing them correctly.

PRECAUTIONS

Please take note of the precautions for each Rite for Life. If you have any concerns with the practise of the Rites in regards to your health please consult your healthcare practitioner. The precautions provided are general, always listen to your own body and take into account that we are all individuals. Each body reacts differently depending on constitutional type, yet generally speaking these precautions are to be noted. As a general rule, do not practise the Rites if you have any knee, back or neck injury. During the practice, if you feel discomfort in the neck, back or knee areas please modify accordingly.

EFFORTLESS EFFORT

With the practice of the *Rites for Life* you will start with seven repetitions, and will build up week by week until you reach 21 repetitions.

Please be aware that by forcing or trying too hard, doing more Rites than what your body is ready for creates blockage. This is why it is very important to listen to your body and to do the level of repetitions that are effortless effort. There is a fine line between pushing yourself too hard and not hard enough. Finding the balance between comfort and being at the point of slight discomfort propels us forward.

As you practise the Rites, which encourage awareness, with time you will know what your perfect level is.

This level changes, and as you increase the repetitions to a level of slight discomfort, this discomfort is only temporary and as soon as they become easy, then you increase. This may take several weeks or months, depending on individuals. It is better that you do not force and rush yourself into reaching 21 repetitions and practise wisely and sustainably to do this practice for life.

RELAXATION

Regardless of how many repetitions you are doing of each Rite, it is vitally important to lie down on the floor completely relaxed at the end of your practice.

Lie on your back, palms facing upward, arms gently by your side a few inches away from the body. Lie with an aligned body, making sure your spine does not arch off the floor by adjusting your pelvis by tilting it so your lower back firmly rests on the floor. If your lower back is still arching off the floor place a pillow under the knees to release the lower back. If your neck arches off the floor place a flat pillow under the head to align the neck with the spine.

CHAPTER 7 tips & consideration for your practise

Now that your body position is aligned and perfectly comfortable affirm to yourself "I am surrender" and allow yourself to completely let go. You can listen to the chakra healing CD during this time, it will enhance your restful healing and prepare you for meditation. This is not only healing energetically, but allows time for the body to assimilate all the exercises as is traditionally done in yoga after a class. It will prepare the mind to be present in time for meditation. Please note this is not a meditation, yet a deep healing relaxation.

chapter 8
embracing your ego

There's a lot of talk about the ego getting in the way of peace, joy and love. After years of unsuccessfully trying to abolish my ego in the quest for enlightenment, I've since learnt to embrace and accept it. With anything in life, I have found that the more you try to get rid of something, the more powerful it becomes.

Your ego is not your enemy if perceived and used in an aware and truthful way. The ego is your mind, body and personality. It's not going anywhere whilst you live a human experience. The ego creates how you see yourself in the world. It's not who you are, yet it's a tool for survival. It ensures you look after your body and achieve things in life with its own agenda usually based on your programming and social conditionings. If it is threatened it will fight for its survival and create a life-long struggle of battle and suffering.

The danger with the ego is allowing it to believe that it is who you are. The ego would like you to think that you are only your mind, body and intellect. By believing this, we lose connection with our true self. Your true self is the part of you that is eternal and is connected to the energies that make up the universe and beyond. This connection is explained in various ways through different religions and philosophies, yet in truth it can only be experienced. An example of this experience is when you are still for a moment in awe of a beautiful sunset. The experience cannot be fully described, only felt. When we are disconnected from our true self because of stress, we become so preoccupied with the outer world that we miss the beauty and magic of life.

Because of the myriad of stresses in the world and in society, and the speed in which we live our life, the ego is overused and has gained too much power. The more power it has, the less people are tapping into their inner consciousness, intuition and awareness. The ego is designed to protect us, but it has a tendency to go overboard.

What we need to do is keep the ego in balance. I've always tried to get rid of my ego but now I've learnt that when the ego is in balance it's connected to who we are. Fully accept the ego, appreciate it as a tool to aid human survival. It will not control or distract your awareness of the perfection of life.

We are now in a world that has advanced to an electronic age with complex economical and social structures that necessitates our modern survival. We have developed creative ways to make life easier in so many wonderful ways. It is obvious now that with the evidence of so much disease, mental illness and stress that we have become humans attached to these devices and lost our connection to the source of nature, which is the source of ourselves.

How many times have you heard the expression, "we are spiritual beings living in human form, we are not the mind, body nor the emotions"? We have forgotten this and instead identify with the outer world of form, our thoughts, feelings and all that is seen.

This is ego; it strongly identifies with its creation, the seen world and all that exists. We have forgotten that the ego was originally designed as a tool for our growth as spiritual beings. We are not the mind, body, emotions; we are magnificent spiritual beings that chose to be here for the expression and experience of simply being. The ego has forgotten its rightful place and led us away from the spiritual, the real to the unreal material world. The unreal is the illusion, the unreal changes constantly and therefore cannot be real. That which is changeable has no truth. Enjoy the game of life, for it has many colours and fluctuates constantly yet the real always remains as love.

As spiritual seekers it is wise not to try to eliminate the ego. Throughout the ages many ancient texts have possibly been misinterpreted to advise this. To place importance on the ego from the perspective of trying to destroy it, is disaster and leads to suffering and stronger identification. On the other hand the cultivation of ego as promoted in today's world has you believing that you require outside circumstances in the form of things and validation from others to be happy. This ultimately leads to wars, competition and disconnection and severe unhappiness.

Acceptance of the ego with a knowing that you are not the ego helps it to let go of power struggles and a need for acknowledgement. The more attention and energy given to it either trying to destroy it or feeding it, gives the ego more power. This is where the game of life becomes interesting; the ego thrives on attention, for either way it does not want to let go. Its nature is to control, it resists the awareness that you are not in truth the ego; it fears its own annihilation. This fear is illusionary for a balanced ego can be a perfect reflection of the Soul.

Our ego's need not be feared and with a loving detached acceptance of the many facets and under the right conditions the ego merges to be an expression of the Divine. To be able to reach this awareness the identification of ego can be shifted to a primary awareness of the Heart, the Seat of the Self. Focusing your primary attention on the heart shifts the energy to the natural state of being, to a wisdom beyond the mind, a universal consciousness of love, peace and joy.

In truth this is all very simple yet we cannot underestimate the power of the ego and its resistance to lose control. It has become a habit over many lifetimes. This strong habitual identification of the ego causes suffering and fortunately for many have become saturated with this suffering and are now becoming very tired and even bored with it. Game over! We have had our fill and through many experiences learned this suffering creates no joy. We can be grateful for all the lessons and live life from our hearts if we choose.

It is important not take this new found awareness for granted and to practise tools that encourage living from the awareness of the Heart, the truth of who you truly are. Constantly clearing the mind, cleansing the emotions, allowing healing for the being as a daily ritual is vitally important. We can never presume that the ego maintains its balance for its nature is to regain control. If we lose our focus and disciplines and fall prey to old habitual conditioned patterns the ego subtly sneaks in. The lesson in life requires a constant awareness of the ego and its games, being mindful always that the real you is in the heart and not in the mind. Cultivating love and joy in daily life is a discipline, never assume if you let that focus slide that you will not become a victim to the games of the ego.

RESISTANCE

The ego is a reality from the human perspective that can be harnessed as awareness grows. In the journey to self-awareness the ego will manipulate the mind into resisting tools that lead to the ego returning to its rightful position as an aid to life and not the god of it.

As we practise self-awareness tools resistance arises. This is the ego's attempt to steer us away from truth and ensure it's own survival. It works through the mind and the chatter becomes insistent in ways of giving many excuses and diversions to the path of greater awareness. It is obvious how controlling it can be and how often we listen to its unwise counsel.

By not resisting the resistance we have a greater chance not to succumb to the aversions of fear the ego embodies. The fear of losing control. One effective way to deal with the resistance is to accept it, simply saying "yes" to it. This has the effect of pacifying the ego by not fighting it and acknowledging its concern. Ultimately the ego as in everything in the universe is energy and all energy really wants is recognition and love. By saying, "yes"- the ego is given the recognition it yearns for and allows a freer flow of energy so the resistance no longer permeates. This in life is so important, by not resisting the urges, desires and diversities we do not give it power.

As soon as you become aware of a thought of resistance say, "yes" to it and with your practice you will become more aware of these resistances that stand in the way of your growth. Resistance is an energy and the nature of it is to flow in and out, express, experience and just like the breath it naturally flows. Saying "yes to resistance" allows it to be, to flow in and flow out.

The same principal extends to all energies, which express themselves as emotions, thoughts, and situations in life. Everything is a flow of energy in the manifested world and once an understanding is attained the experience is one of a flow in and out. Life is an experience of all facets of energy to be embraced and learnt from. The nature of evolution is to move forward, to progress with greater awareness. This progression flows without unnecessary angst and suffering.

The ego has advantage in today's world of stress and disconnection; it uses the lack of awareness caused by these stresses to take greater hold. As mentioned before the importance of getting in touch with nature and re-connecting within is far more urgent today than ever before and hence the importance of practising tools of self-mastery like *Rites for Life* that disable the power of resistance, fear and wanting of ego.

The ego which expresses itself as the mind wants to analyse, to understand the why, how and when of life's circumstances. Allow yourself to trust in your inner wisdom, knowing that the answers to your enquiries are not in your mind.

How can the mind possibly know anything in the concerns of consciousness? Firstly, the mind is a conditioned program exactly like your computer. It only has the information that you programmed into it. The mind reacts and responds to information computed. The awareness and universal intelligence is beyond the mind. It is futile to ask the mind anything relating to truth, it does not know. The mind is a useful tool for referencing phone numbers, dates, information that has been taught and registered to be used for our human survival. Beyond the mind is intuition and as awareness grows intuition seeds start to sprout.

Re-learning to trust what feels good without the need for logical or scientific explanation leads to this intuitive knowing. Energetic feelings are tangible, thought and reason are conceptual. It has been said by the wise ones that no truth is found in concept. Concepts are mind created. Learn to cultivate inner knowing by feeling the feelings and not listening to thoughts and doubts of the mind. It is said that where there is confusion there can be no Truth. Saying "yes to confusion" helps the mind to stop the merry-go-round madness of questioning.

SURRENDER

So far, attention to the emotional and mental/ego processes for healing and clearing have been discussed. As awareness expands it shifts its vibration to the spiritual dimension.

When intuition transcends the mind, it follows with a natural progression to a higher dimension of pure consciousness, which allows a surrendered state of being.

Surrender is the spiritual healing and cleansing tool that may activate the ego's resistances and fears. This may happen when the concept is first introduced. The mind has a fear based conditioned response to letting go and believes that to surrender is to give up, hands in the air to the enemy. It brings up feelings of giving your power away. Yes, surrender does suggest this, yet not in the way the mind may think.

The spiritual meaning is simply that Surrender is an attitude that allows all that stands in the way of your beautiful Divine Self to flow out. It encourages the letting go of all the conditioned, programmed garbage, the concepts that result in all forms of suffering.

Surrendering to something or someone outside of yourself is not true surrender. We need not give up or give away anything to anyone or anything, whether that be to a religion, belief system, philosophy, guru, leader, parent, child, lover or friend. Surrendering within and not without is the crucial difference. Surrendering to the truth of being, to your inner wisdom, to your heart, may pleasantly surprise you for life without obstruction creates harmonious perfection without doing, trying or manipulating. It just flows as nature intended.

chapter 9
your heart's purpose

The *Rites for Life* clear the path to knowing your true purpose. It is the heart that holds the knowledge of your purpose. The yogis have known for thousands of years that the heart holds more information than the brain.

We are conditioned to search the brain for answers yet the mind is only a limited program, like a computer. The brain can only give the information that has been programmed into it. The heart has a greater awareness and knowing than the brain, so the way to discover your true purpose is through the heart.

The *Rites for Life* can help to unleash a greater awareness of what you are here to do in life by opening up the heart chakra. Many people have lost touch with their passion and are disconnected with their own path because they identify more with their brain than their heart. This can cause feelings of apathy and lack of interest in life.

After you have been practising the *Rites for Life* it unravels these feelings of dispassion and awakens a knowing of what you are here to do. In order to live your life with purpose here are some helpful tools and guidelines that you can apply.

VISION

You will start to have a vision or concept of what it is you are here to do. Think about what you are most passionate about and often these will be your greatest gifts to share with the world. To have an attitude of being in service is not being a martyr, it is having the ability to share your gifts with passion. Being in service really means that you give unconditionally and this is deeply satisfying and the key to success. It is important to firstly be in service to yourself and your vision, and then you have the capacity to be in service to others.

Trust the vision and hold it firmly in your heart. It is not necessary to be specific with endless details, but to be clear on the bigger picture, for example love, health and success. This is not to say that you will not get the big house and the nice car but that you will be provided perfectly according to your vision. Don't get bogged down in the details for the Universe knows how and when to deliver.

DESIRE

The Rites will help your inner desire to be re-awakened with a strong energy of excitement about your vision. Allow yourself to feel this all-consuming desire. For this desire to manifest, according to Universal Laws, it must be aligned with your higher purpose. It is possible to manifest with a focused energy anything you desire, but for it to be sustainable and fulfilling it needs to be your heart's desire, not your desire. This then makes it really clear as to what is true.

BELIEVE

Often what inhibits us from our inherit fulfillment is not believing that we deserve it or that we doubt it is possible. Allow yourself the belief that it is possible; in fact fulfillment is your birthright. Belief is a concept that can cast doubt and fear aside. Replace negative doubt with positive belief as this raises your energies. If you believe in something strongly enough that is aligned with your true purpose then this belief eventually develops into a knowing.

ACCEPTANCE

Accept your vision is your true purpose. Sometimes your true vision may surprise you. I've known high-level corporates who were terribly dissatisfied even though they were highly successful. Once they started the *Rites for Life* they changed careers completely, at first with trepidation but with an acceptance of their vision they found fulfilling happiness and greater health. Likewise I've known housewives who practised the *Rites for Life* launch their own business fulfilling their vision. Accept your vision and know that it's revealing your path.

ACTION

Act like you already are what you want or what you are meant to be. For instance if you have an illness and you would like your birthright of health act as if you are already healthy. This will ensure that you do the things that promote good health. It will also ensure you speak, live, walk, and breathe as a healthy person. Practising the *Rites for Life* is an example of taking action towards living your vision.

DETACH

Once you have your vision, and a strong burning desire to fulfill your purpose, and a knowing that it is possible, and the action that is required to live that purpose, let it go. Surrender any attachment to the outcome utterly and unconditionally. Let go of the need to understand how. Give up reason and conditioned logical thinking so as not to be trapped in the mind. Have no expectation of how or when it is to be. Let go in the knowing that providing your vision is aligned with your higher purpose that it is already done. The universe will reflect the same energy back to you of what you live. Detachment is letting go of the outcome, but not the action.

For example if it is a healthy body that is your vision, continue to do all that a healthy body does but let go of the end result. Know that you are perfect now, and the awareness of every single cell of your body will synchronise to the message of perfection. By focusing on the outcome you are focused on the future, which never comes. Here and now you are perfect.

chapter 10
rites for life program

This program is a guideline on how to practise your Rites safely. Take into account that you are an individual and that you practise at your own pace. Many people find that to do the full program takes longer yet it is imperative that regardless of how fit you are not to finish the program in less time than you need.

WEEK 1-9 RITES 1-5	• 7 repetitions of each rite daily for 2 weeks • Add 2 repetitions of each rite every week until reaching 21 repetitions • At the completion of your daily program proceed to the daily relaxation CD or do the chakra relaxation
WEEK 9-12 RITES 1-5	• Continue 21 repetitions of the 5 rites daily for 3 weeks • Rites 1-5 will take approximately 10 minutes per day to complete • At the completion of your daily program proceed to the daily relaxation CD or do the chakra relaxation
WEEK 12-21 RITE 6	• Complete your daily rites 1-5 of 21 repetitions then add rite 6 • Start with 7 repetitions for 2 weeks • Add 2 repetitions every week until reaching 21 repetitions in 9 weeks • At the completion of your daily program proceed to the daily relaxation CD or do the chakra relaxation
WEEK 21-30 RITE 7	• Complete your daily rites 1-6 of 21 repetitions then add rite 7 • Start with 7 repetitions for 2 weeks • Add 2 repetitions every 1 week until reaching 21 repetitions in 9 weeks • At the completion of your daily program proceed to the daily relaxation CD or do the chakra relaxation
WEEK 30 RITE 8	• You have successfully learnt the Rites for Life • From this point 21 repetitions of all the rites are practised • Refer to the meditation CD when completing your daily rites • The experience of the Rites for Life and meditation is a daily program of 40 minutes

rite 1
SPINNING

rite 2
LEG RAISES

rite 5
DOWNWARD DOG / UPWARD DOG

rite 6
FORWARD BEND TWIST

CHAPTER 10 rites for life program

rite 3
BACK ARCH

rite 4
TABLE TOP

rite 7
WIDE LEGGED HEAD STAND

rite 8
SMILING MEDITATION

chapter 11
case studies

Sally

Sally came to a yoga class and decided to do the Rites for Life workshop. She was young and very stressed. Sally was an old soul who was very confused about the wisdom she had. She connected to the energy of the Rites for Life and started to open up in ways that gave expression to her wisdom. Her body, although young, needed more strength. She was naturally flexible and found that she would visit a chiropractor twice a week to alleviate her back condition and to realign her spine because she constantly threw the alignment out due to lack of muscle strength and tone.

As she practised the Rites for Life at home daily, the visits to the chiropractor ceased and this young woman became truly beautiful; the way she was meant to be. She continued to come to yoga so I could see the unraveling in her week after week, year after year. All these years later we stay in contact. I am honoured to know a very special soul that often assisted my in workshops and was of great service to others. She moved away, married, had a stunning natural birth child and is dedicated to the Conscious Parenting Movement.

Anna

Anna was a stay-at-home mum with an interest in the alternative industry. She was concerned about attending the workshop for she was scheduled to have a minor operation to remove an ovarian cyst. She asked me if she should put the operation off until after the Workshop. I advised her that it was her decision to make so not to influence her in any way. She decided to brave it for there was understandably a lot of fear associated with her health. To this day she still talks about the amazing transformation.

After the Rites for Life workshop she visited the specialist to determine the state of her cyst. She called me very excited that the cyst had completely disappeared and found it be a miracle. When these healings occur it is not my place to analyse the hows, although I do know that the energy transmutes during the practice release, that which is ready to be released. Anna had a lot of fear and fear does create blockage. The Rites activated the release.

Anna went on to study massage, developed a successful practice and continued the pursuit to help others by training as a yoga teacher. She has a yoga school and writes about the most fascinating topics associated with the language of words. She promotes the Rites and has passed on many of her students to the workshops. I am grateful to know this wonderful woman.

Mary

Mary was a young corporate executive, with a sunny disposition and high anxiety. She came to classes and booked into the workshop. Her energy was always one of giving and very respectful of the teachings. She struggled with self-confidence yet had so much to offer. A wise soul beneath her phobias. Practising the Rites for Life lead her to leave her stressful job, venture out on her own to establish a highly successful business in coaching large corporations change their dynamics of self serving competition to respecting individual talents and strengths by working together for the good of the whole. She leads by example and has profited the lives of many individuals and companies.

She has assisted me with many workshops and continues to grow and shine to that of an enlightened soul. We have a joke between us, and I say to her not to shine too brightly for it is blinding me. A true treasure in my life and for all those around her. She would not be without her daily practice for she knows her disciplines are the key to her business and personal success. The added benefit to her was that she is fitter than ever before and even more beautiful, full of joy.

Simon

Simon was a Health Spa Manager and Co-ordinator. He came to yoga like many others and took to the Rites for Life with an almost fierce determination. At first he was releasing uncomfortably and then we discovered he was doing far too many repetitions for he misunderstood the instructions. In his mind he could not fathom that initially a 10-minute practice could achieve the benefits purported. He practised for an hour.

Bless him, he was so enthusiastic and over did it. After the correction he had a sense of relief for he was experiencing some very cathartic reactions that were difficult to manage. His emotions were out of control and he did not know what was happening. He continued a correct practice, his emotions stabilised and found that his spine improved dramatically; it was stronger and far more flexible. The flexibility in his whole body improved and was incredibly noticeable in yoga classes.

This lovely man returned to do the workshops many times. I suggested that he did not need to any more, so he offered to assist to continue to remind himself of the benefits. His mind, having been highly analytical, wanting to know the reason behind everything, became more at peace and as his awareness grew, he came to experience surrender, surrender of the cluttered mind which stood in the way of his self discovery.

A year later he asked to be trained as a yoga teacher. He is now a well-known and respected yoga teacher that has far more depth and understanding than the many modern body driven yoga trends of today. He is a very generous friend and helps many on their path of yoga with in-depth understanding of physiology and philosophy. He lives his passion and would not be without his practice of the Rites for Life.

Peter

I had a regular large class every Saturday morning for nearly 20 years and one morning a gentleman came, unsteady on his feet and smelled to high heaven of alcohol. You can imagine what the yoga students thought. He managed to get through the class paid me and left. This happened many times and some students complained about his attendance and asked me to ask him to leave. I explained that if he chose to come and was obviously needing help through the yoga practice and healing meditation at the end of the class that we all had to cast aside our judgements and welcome him like any other.

The workshop was scheduled and to my surprise he booked in. This man came with such attentiveness and a big smile that added to the energy of the day. This time he was not inebriated. Peter continued to come and his appearance freshened up with a light that shone from within him. One evening I answered the phone to an elderly woman's voice who claimed to be in his mother. She called to thank me for returning her beautiful son back to himself. His wife and children were delighted by the changes in him. She told me it had saved his life.

Peter felt the energy in his body and regained a faith in life and continues to this day to smile and see the divinity in himself and all those around him. Imagine if I would of sent him away for he was challenging especially to the others. He had lost his connection to the universal all and by practising the Rites released his blockages and really felt his energy, the universal energy, which he now knows, is one with. Every time I think of him it makes me smile with gratitude to Peter and all that he taught us and thank him for bravely turning up.

CHAPTER 11 case studies

A book of testimonies could easily be filled with so many transformations purported. The only way to transform yourself to a greater, truer version is to just do them.

Now that you have read this book, allow yourself to open your heart and even allow yourself to learn and practise these profoundly healing tools. Then experience yourself unfolding day by day so that you become a living testament of an open heart that lives and breathes love in every moment of your life.

Now surely that is our Divine Purpose, the infinite reason for being. We are here to enlighten the path of the Divine!

namaste

RITES FOR LIFE
REGENERATE | MASTER ENERGY | TRANSFORM

For further information contact Anne Lewis
email **info@ritesforlife.com** or phone **+61 409 976 075**
www.ritesforlife.com

www.ingramcontent.com/pod-product-compliance
Lightning Source LLC
Chambersburg PA
CBHW041620220426
43661CB00049B/1547